On Stage

On Stage
The Theatrical Dimension of Video Image

Mathilde Roman

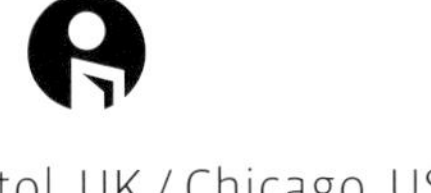

intellect Bristol, UK / Chicago, USA

First published in the UK in 2016 by
Intellect, The Mill, Parnall Road, Fishponds, Bristol, BS16 3JG, UK

First published in the USA in 2016 by
Intellect, The University of Chicago Press, 1427 E. 60th Street,
Chicago, IL 60637, USA

Original title *On Stage: La dimension scénique de l'image vidéo.*
© Edition en langue française, 2012, Le Gac Press. Translated from
the French by Charles Penwarden.

A catalogue record for this book is available from the
British Library.

Copy-editor: MPS Technologies
Cover designer: Stephanie Sarlos
Cover image: Inspired by 4brane from Laurent Grasso
Production manager: Jelena Stanovnik
Typesetting: Contentra Technologies

Print ISBN: 978-1-78320-580-6
ePDF ISBN: 978-1-78320-581-3
ePUB ISBN: 978-1-78320-582-0

Printed and bound by Hobbs, UK

Published in collaboration with Muse, Monaco

m u s e

cultural publishing
monaco

Contents

Preface

Two features make Mathilde Roman's work exceptional, and particularly useful for scholars of contemporary art, critics and general readers: its theoretical angle and its critical precision. First, the special angle the author has chosen is the theatricality of video installation. This is partly a reflection on the medium's specificity, partly, and more relevantly in my view, on the specificity of the practices of the medium as most frequently encountered today. Like the theatre, installation is characterized by space, time and fictionality. The spatio-temporality of video implies movement, comparable to actors' movements on stage. Moreover, like a stage, installations are sculptural, their settings architectural. And due to the fictionality inherent even in documentary video, they produce an immersive effect. This effect is multisensorial, as the visitor or viewer finds herself both inside the scenes on the videos and inside the space of the installation. As an art historian, Roman draws on early-twentieth century precedents in experimental theatre to provide the contemporary medium with a history. As an active art critic, she provides it with concrete cases that bring the practices of the medium to the reader's doorstep. This is the second aspect that makes this book so valuable.

Travelling through a wide range of cases, readers experience Roman's first-hand immersion in the installations she has visited. The author's skill in describing installations vividly with a minimal amount of words makes the book a joy to read. One feels almost present inside the installations she describes, places theoretically, and evaluates in one big sweep. Some of the most prominent artists of today are evoked and engaged with, while many less widely known artists join forces to create an epic tableau of practices some of which a reader may have seen, but more likely, can get to know through these wonderful descriptions. An astute critic, Roman writes in concrete, lucid prose, avoiding jargon and long theoretical developments. Her swift brush strokes make the reading extremely pleasant, without sacrificing depth to speed.

The way installations of multiple screens occupy space with their time-bound images of bodies orienting the viewer's gaze, for example, is limpidly exposed through a close reading of works by David Claerbout and Julian Rosefeldt, two artists so different that any hasty generalization is skilfully pre-empted. Meanwhile, the issue of the body and its presence/ absence is already introduced, to be further developed in a later chapter. The way video engages the theatre is explained along with acute evocations of artists whose work challenges traditional elements such as character and 'real' space. In video installation inhabiting a situation becomes inhabiting the stage, but the crucial verb is 'inhabiting', rather than, say, 'watching'. I won't go on to enumerate all the topics that the author introduces, almost casually, without didactic insistence but rather, through the practices that bring them alive.

Video installation as a medium or genre in contemporary art is as richly represented on the art scene as it is poorly studied. At least, in the integrated theoretical and critical perspectives presented here. Therefore, Mathilde Roman's study is very welcome in the international scholarship on the arts. There are some companions for it, but not much of the same calibre and angle. Among the few exceptions I can mention Janna Houwen, *Mapping Moving Media*, Münster, Germany: LIT (in press). This book is theoretically and critically very rich, but is less focused on installation per se. Its systematic comparison between film and video provides a very valuable backdrop for Roman's positioning of the medium in relation to the theatre. My own book, *Thinking in Film: The Politics of Video Installation According to Eija-Liisa Ahtila*, London, UK: Bloomsbury (2013), offers theoretical reflections, anchored in Henri Bergson's philosophy of the image as always already in movement, in dialogue with a single artist's work. These two books can be considered a setting, to stay in this book's vocabulary, upon which Roman's unique text can move, and move us. That the book is a pleasure to read adds to its merit as a contribution to scholarship. For, what use is scholarship if it does not convince those who are the primary judges of art; the actual viewers who see, experience and assess the way the artworks change their perspective on the world.

Mieke Bal

Introduction

Outside the Frame

In 1961, the Brazilian artist, Hélio Oiticica, stated, 'the age of the end of the tableau' (…) 'definitively begun' by leaving behind the frame, because 'painting had to leave the tableau, be completed in space, not in appearance or superficially, but in its profound integrity'.[1] He started making installations in which the painted canvas was part of a greater whole, filling space and freeing itself of the picture wall, moving outside what, for centuries, had been its assigned place. Oiticica was far from isolated in his approach. His direction was symptomatic of the movement affecting painting generally, shifting it elsewhere, upsetting its codes. More generally, the 1960s were a period characterized by the need to escape, symbolically or literally, the usual territories of art, to set out on a quest for new tools, new spaces and to question frontiers.

This was the period when artists started using video in an approach advocating a spilling over of established loci, especially those of television and cinema. There were numerous experiments in diverting and re-appropriating existing forms; and at the same time, other spaces were invented for the image. It was not long before, in Oiticica's words, video 'completed itself in space', existing beyond the monitor. Artists addressed the question of reception by dealing directly with the space and temporality of the exhibition. Nam June Paik, Peter Campus, Dan Graham and many others intensified our relation to the moving image by integrating it into sculptural work, conceiving it for specific spaces, playing with what was out of the frame, dismembering the screen, opening the frame and creating multiple time frames. They thus worked towards the end of a certain regime of the image by inscribing the need to confront space within its 'profound integrity'. The work escaped its assigned spaces, the wall and the base, and sought out other regimes of presence. Experiments took up the tradition of other efforts to extend beyond art, from Futurism and Dadaism to performance and Land Art. Video and artists' films are forms that reach beyond the frame of the image, and it is their porosity that enabled them to become a major field of contemporary creation. The linkages and excesses that they affect concern, in particular, the exhibition and theatrical space.

The Theatricality of the Visual Work

Relations between the visual arts and the performing arts have always been complex, and their history is marked by a number of major collaborations, such as that of the renowned Ballets Russes in the early twentieth century, or, in the 1960s, the artistic undertakings around the

Judson Church and Black Mountain College, but also by instances of mutual mistrust. The Renaissance principle of *ut pictura poesis*, after the formula by Horace, may have affirmed the richness of comparisons between the artists, but on this view, the value of painting lay in its relation to poetry. In the eighteenth century, Lessing analysed the difference between the two genres, their relation to the imagination and to the signs used for representation. Where painting is an ordering of bodies in space, poetry is composed in time. This conception, which creates a hierarchy of values, implies that attempts to create a dialogue between disciplines are debasing, or alienating. This model was forcefully rejected in the early twentieth century by the Dadaists, but the principle of mixing different arts was not really accepted until several decades later. According to the idea put forward by Hal Foster in his essay, 'The Return of the Real', which is based on the temporal conception of subjectivity in Freud, the history of art is 'a continual process of protension and retension, a complex relay of anticipated futures and reconstructed pasts—in short, in a deferred action that throws over any simple scheme of before and after, cause and effect, origin and repetition'.[2] Having emerged in the 1920s, the idea of the need to think the qualities of the performing and visual arts, to inscribe the museum-based artwork in a spatio-temporal dimension, was forgotten until it reappeared in the 1960s, and then became firmly established with the practice of the installation in the 1990s, once the traumatic moments of the encounter between the arts had been gradually digested. In a very illuminating article, 'La colonne relevée', Giovanni Parenzan focuses on one of these moments, in 1961, when a show by the Living Theater in New York ended with a *Column* by Robert Morris falling on the stage.[3] This event, a strong precursor of the productive encounter between the spaces of the stage and of sculpture, was long untold, until it was re-appropriated by a whole tendency in contemporary art that asserted the theatrical dimension of the visual work.

If, today, this development is widely accepted, the appropriation of the qualities traditionally attributed to the stage by the visual arts initially met with intense criticism. The American art historian and theoretician Michael Fried was the emblematic figure of this opposition to the new tendency. In 1967, he critiqued the tendency of artworks to enter a regime of theatricality, which as he saw it was embodied by Minimalism.[4] He inveighed against the 'the same general, enveloping, infectious theatricality that corrupted literalist sensibility in the first place and in the grip of which the developments in question—and modernist painting in general—are seen as nothing more than an uncompelling and presenceless kind of theatre', going so far as to assert, 'The success, even the survival, of the arts has come increasingly to depend on their ability to defeat theatre'.[5] He rightly describes the Minimalist tendency as an art that is constituted around the time of the stage, that of duration, involving the beholder in an immersive relation that is psychological and sensorial. He contrasts this with the reflexivity of the modernist work, with its 'present-ness', its 'instantaneousness', and critiques its non-autonomous nature. By inscribing itself in the time of experience, in the beholder's expectations, the Minimalist work engages a spatio-temporal reception that takes it far from the traditional status of the artwork. Fried's article, which generated much enduring critical debate, went against the creative tendency of the day and revealed, above all, the direction that it was about to take, increasingly taking over the exhibition space as a kind of stage. For example, in his *Bedroom Ensemble* (1963), Claes Oldenburg placed objects together in such a way as to create a theatrical space, which visitors were then encouraged to move around in. The sculptural work was no longer isolated from its context but, instead, affirmed its temporal nature, its relation to the present, to history, in opposition to the classical definition of the ideal timelessness of the artwork. Writing of this development and the issues behind it, Patricia Falguières notes, 'The conceptual moment of art in the 1970s is the coincidence of the subtraction of the artist (making into an effigy is a local version of "the death of the author," there are others) with an extreme theatricalization of the agencies of art. More than ever, art as either a genre or category is identified with a theatrical space. The "field of art," a sociological category, is approached theatrically, resulting in an 'art of the stage"'.[6]

It is interesting to note, however, that for Fried there is one artistic form that is saved from this theatrical tendency. This is cinema that 'escapes theatre—automatically, as it were' and therefore 'provides a welcome and absorbing refuge to sensibilities at war with theatre and theatricality'.[7] For Fried, this 'automatic, guaranteed character of the refuge is a structural quality of the medium' rather than a modernist choice. My argument here, however, is that the theatricalization of art is embodied in an artistic form that is directly linked to cinema: video.

The Video Installation: Closeness to the Stage

Installation is a word commonly used to designate a work that appropriates the space in which it is exhibited; a work in which a relation to its setting is an integral part of a formal proposition that carries a total aesthetic experience. By extension, the term video installation is used for a work combining a video with a sculptural proposition. It is an exploration of the artistic field, designated as an 'art of the stage', by means of video, creating an environment in which the image is integrated. The apparatus for exhibiting the animated image, be it a monitor, a screen or a simple ray of light, is conceived as creating aesthetic conditions to be explored. These works take up position in space and time by affirming their dialogue with stage-based forms such as theatre, performance, dance and even concerts. This closeness also derives from the history of the theatre, in which light and image technologies were quick to occupy the space of the stage. As analysed by Béatrice Picon-Vallin, following on from Adolphe Appia and his use of light as a dramaturgical device, the English director and theoretician of theatrical art, Edward Gordon Craig, began putting screens on stage as of 1907. 'These could be coloured by the light and, although he did not think of them as potential surfaces for projection, he had established the principle of a stage comprising a multiplicity of moving screens, which would later take shape in the project for "a thousand stages in one"'.[8] Interplay between moving images and theatre developed in the 1920s and became truly substantial in the 1960s, consequently questioning the status of each medium.

By taking to the space of the stage, video affirmed its spatial and temporal nature, its play with on-screen and off-screen and with illusion and what it enables. Its presence questions the actor's body and modifies theatrical space. This close connection between theatre and video art, which is now substantial, reveals the closeness of their respective treatments of the space and time of representation.[9] The introduction of video on stage does not necessarily stem from a desire to create a total work of art, not in the Wagnerian sense of the *Gesamtkunstwerk*, but as something that partakes of an exploration of theatrical space. In the same way, the theatrical dimension of the video installation does not lead to the creation of a total show within the museum space, but to the affirmation of a specificity of a visual language that I shall try to define in the study that follows.

From the outset, then, video was a major actor in the spectacle in its various contexts, on the theatre stage but also in the spaces of entertainment in consumer societies. Charles and Ray Eames, for example, produced impressive multi-screen environments to present their films about the American way of life at fairs. For the Moscow World's Fair of 1959, they conceived a set-up with seven big screens creating an immersive experience for visitors. The film they showed, *Glimpses of the USA*, constituted of 'More than 2,200 still and moving images (some from Billy Wilder's *Some Like it Hot*) presenting "a typical work day" in the life of the United States in nine minutes and "a typical weekend day" in three minutes'.[10] This spectacular device was a great popular success, prompting the Eameses to develop such presentations further, as at the 1964 World's Fair in New York, where *Think* was projected on fourteen screens in the IBM module designed by the Saarinen office. The screens were of different sizes, spread across a spherical space that totally enveloped the viewer. Access was via a hydraulic elevator, the idea being to give visitors an experience off the ground and outside the usual spatial and temporal coordinates. The gaze was completely surrounded by images, not only in the profusion of the fast-paced editing, but also in the simultaneous multiplicity on the screens. In her important study of the Eameses' filmic pieces, Béatriz Colomina notes that in *Think* 'The eye cannot escape the screens and each screen is bordered by other screens'.[11] The Eameses' contribution to the history of projection apparatus is interesting because it was developed in the context of fairs, and set up a hypnotic relation of fascination that would be exploited by the commercial and cultural industries. Today, no event, be it commercial, didactic, economic or political, is conceivable without video projections. Screens are everywhere and if, in 1959, the Eames showed a precocious understanding of the form as a resource for communication, using them today in an artistic project demands, on the contrary, a real sense of distance in relation to its mechanisms of seduction.

Exploring the spatiality of video has become a central creative domain in contemporary art. Artists use multiple supports, construct new kinds of montage in which images are juxtaposed in space, obliging the viewer to truly engage in their relation to the moving image. In an exhibition context, the video image is inventing new devices that are bringing about a revolution in the way we look at a work. Its visual, aural and temporal materials make it a locus that is especially interesting for analysing the evolution of artistic experience and, more generally, our developing relation to images since the 1960s. Immersive processes mean that the spectator is consciously aware of her receptive state and, by means of structures that shift our relation to the image, the artists I discuss here, who are major, contemporary actors in this history, will enable us to reflect on the approaches and issues underpinning video productions installed in space.

Notes

1 Hélio Oiticica, *Aspiro ao Grande Labirinto*, Rio de Janeiro: Rocco, 1986, published in *Hélio Oiticica*, Galerie Nationale du Jeu de Paume, Paris, and Witte de With, Roterdam, 1992.
2 Hal Foster, *The Return of the Real*, Cambridge: Mass. MIT Press, 1996.
3 Giovanni Parenzan, 'La colonne relevée', Agôn (online), no. 2: 'L'accident'. http//w7.ens-lsh.fr/agon/index.php?id=1062
4 'Art and Objecthood', *Artforum*, 1967.
5 'Art and Objecthood', *Artforum*, 1967.
6 Patricia Falguières, 'Aire de jeu', *Les Cahiers du Musée National d'Art Moderne*, no. 101, Paris, autumn 2007, p. 65.
7 Patricia Falguières, 'Aire de jeu', *Les Cahiers du Musée National d'Art Moderne*, no. 101, Paris, autumn 2007, p. 65.
8 Béatrice Picon-Vallin, 'Les dispositifs vidéo en question: histoire et actualité', *Le Pavillon*, no. 3, Monaco, École d'Art et de Scénographie, 2011, p. 28–37.
9 On this point, see the two volumes edited by Béatrice Picon-Vallin, *Les écrans sur scène* (L'Age d'Homme, 1998) and *La scène et les images* (CNRS Arts du Spectacle, 2001).
10 Béatriz Colomina, 'Enclosed by Images. The Eameses' Multimedia Architecture', in Tanya Leighton (ed.), *Art and the Moving Image, a Critical Reader*, Tate Publishing and Afterall, London, 2008, p. 77.
11 Béatriz Colomina, 'Enclosed by Images. The Eameses' Multimedia Architecture' in Tanya Leighton (ed.), *Art and the Moving Image, a Critical Reader*, Tate Publishing and Afterall, 2008, p. 87.

Chapter 1

A Stage for the Image: Occupying Space, Multiple Screens

During the 1920s, the Russian avant-garde artist El Lissitzky, who taught at the Bauhaus, conceived spatial apparatuses in which painting and sculpture together reached beyond their assigned place to constitute total artworks, inviting the viewer to move around and manipulate them. In the spirit of the experiments being made at the same time by Vladimir Tatlin in his *Konterrelief* and Kurt Schwitters in his *Merzbau*, he created a new way of uniting the space of the work with the space of its presentation. The *Abstract Cabinet* (1927–28) that he created for Alexander Dorner at the Landesmuseum in Hannover was a revolutionary conception and art historical landmark. Its display gave spatial extension to the pictorial researches of Malevich, Mondrian, Moholy-Nagy, Baumeister, Van Doesburg, Gabo and Lissistzky, brought together by an enlightened curator. The visitor was confronted with works that defied the flatness of the wall, positioned within a display device (sliding panels) that he was asked to activate, thereby engaging with other modalities of reception. El Lissitzky's position was radical: 'Space: that which is not looked at through a keyhole, not through an open door. Space does not exist for the eye only: it is not a picture; one wants to live in it'.[1] He sought to wrest viewers from their passivity with regard to artworks and make them active in the process of their perception. This project, which was also political in an age when capitalist society had started to anchor the individual in a consumerist relation to goods and images, has numerous echoes in today's world.

Artists have made abundant use of the immersive resources offered by new technologies to create artistic experiences pursuing the direction mapped out by El Lissitzky, inviting viewers to enter the space of the work both physically and mentally, to inhabit it for the duration of their visit, and even to activate it when interactivity is used. By affirming the connection between the stage and the exhibition gallery, video installation makes the viewer an actor who moves around between the works and whose experience of reception becomes performative. Entering the space of projection, we are immersed in an imaginary that, while constructed in and by the image, also exceeds the image. Walking around the screens, deciding to stop or keep moving, to sit or to stand, to look at one work or at several, to isolate or move the images round, to listen or to put the headphones back—all these choices allow the beholder to choose their perceptual position with regard to the works, while plunging them into an immersion that can often be destabilizing. Françoise Parfait has highlighted this aspect in her study of video installations, 'Disorientation is one of the stumbling blocks of the spatio-temporal experience offered the visitor, often beginning with physical disorientation and ending in a mental disorientation conducive to thinking about the conditions of perception and language'.[2] The structure of the video installation, with its ability to combine moving images, the spatialization of sound and architectural devices, offers a privileged space for thinking about our relation to representation. By peopling the exhibition space with works that go beyond the framework of the image, David Claerbout, Julian Rosefeldt, Ugo Rondinone and Sebastian Diaz Morales offer immersive, stimulating experiences of seeing that are constantly calling attention to the relation to the body and the gaze that is their underpinning. Through them there emerges a way of thinking about perception and a questioning of the relations to the world that subtend it.

David Claerbout: Porous Temporalities

Because of its aural dimension, artists and curators often prefer to show video work in closed, isolated spaces, commonly known as the *black box*, imitating the cinema. This immersion in darkness helps the spectator to concentrate by keeping out unwanted interference. By creating a projection space that, in contrast, allows light around the screen, and by letting the sound contaminate the general atmosphere of the room, David Claerbout (Belgium, born 1969) is one of these artists who are questioning our relation to the moving image.

Moving into a Claerbout installation, one is struck by the silence, the appearance of immobility, as if time were suspended. One treads more discreetly, not to escape but in response to the rhythm emanating from the work. The image inhabits the space, marking it with its distended temporality, in a coming and going between photographic fixity and the motion of video. There is something fundamental about the interstice into which this artist inserts his practice, in that it is all a matter of questioning and, above all, metamorphosing, the paradoxical impression that we have when looking at a photograph. The fixed image of a past moment is the sign that something *has been*, but this certainty also brings discomfort because of the gaping holes that, at the same time, we open in our memory's outer reaches. In his works, Claerbout offers to prise open the density of time, to reanimate dead things. We are far from the action of desacralization or, on the contrary, resurrection. The images chosen by the artist are not icons before which we lament their loss; they are resplendently banal: breakfast al fresco, a tree, a couple dancing, a motorway interchange. Each piece is autonomous, has its own alchemy of discreet movement and light allowing uncertainty to creep in with great subtlety. We are immersed in the movements of the leaves of a tree, arrested by the eyes of a little girl who turns her head and greets us, struck by the projected image of a man and woman dancing.

Experiencing the works is key to understanding how installations are never closed in on themselves. The exhibition space is porous, the installations open to one another, the partitions between them full of holes; these panels act not to separate but to create ricochets, playing on transparency and opacity in order to avoid the isolation of works that one would like to appreciate in their continuity and diversity, which is the drawback of the conventional display apparatus. This is how Claerbout describes the layout of his 2007 solo show at the Pompidou Centre in Paris,

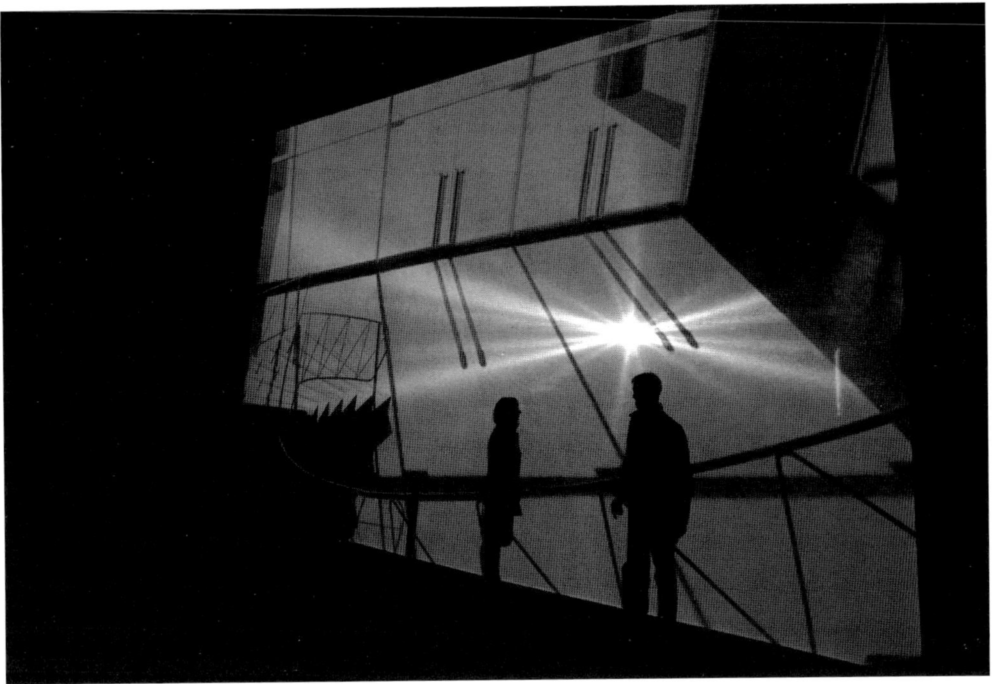

David Claerbout, *Shadow Piece*, 2005. Installation view at Pompidou Center, Paris, 2007. Photo: Georges Meguerditchian. Courtesy of the artist.

Here [...] the spectator enters through a dark space painted black. On the way in they are confronted with one of the works in the exhibition, *Shadow Piece*, projected onto a translucent screen. When they pass through the screen, everything is in white, transparent, with no constructed 'cube' to disrupt the gaze.[3]

The whole exhibition is thus conceived as a great stage on which projections are articulated. The picture walls/screens structure the space but do not close it, as they are always traversed by light. In the work that confronts visitors as they enter, *Shadow Piece* (2005), a film shows people walking past a glass building that they are unable to enter, whereas their shadows can. This visual effect created by means of two distinct shots echoes the viewer's position with regard to the exhibition. They too can walk between images but never enter their place, while their mind can, like a shadow, become sucked into the projected territories. For Claerbout, the handling of sound is particularly important as a means of avoiding confusion. Like the images, the sounds coexist and do not need to be isolated. This gives the viewer the sensation of being on an open stage where signs appear as and when they move around, cohering and coming apart as they do so. In some pieces, headphones allow visitors to listen to a dialogue and those accede to another level of interpretation. Benches placed around

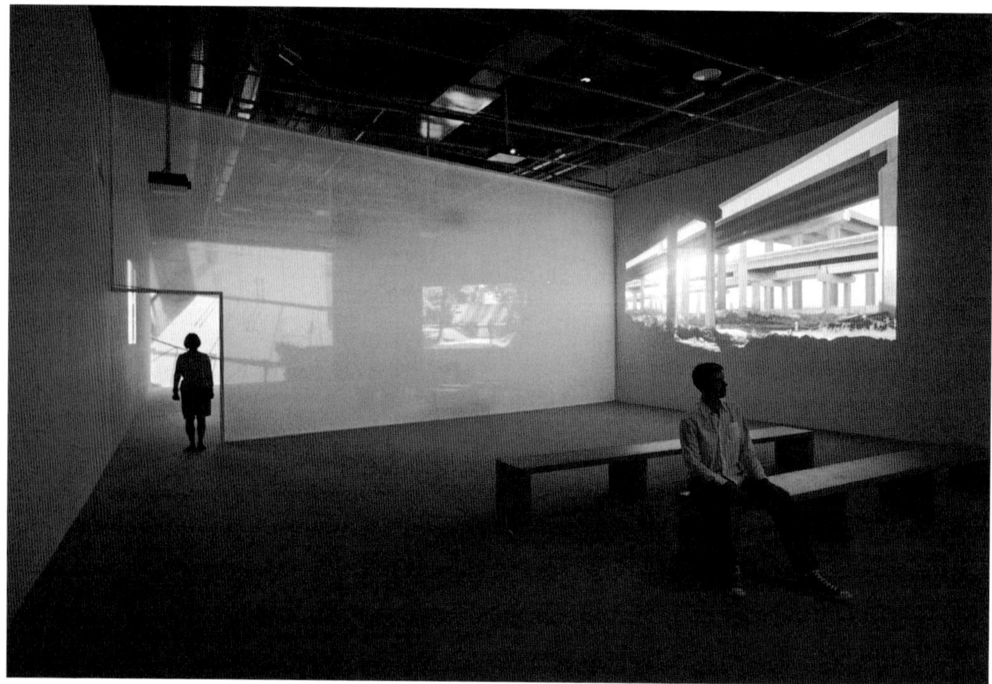

David Claerbout. Installation view at Pompidou Center, Paris, 2007. Photo: Georges Meguerditchian. Courtesy of the artist.

the exhibition invite participants to settle and become drawn into the images, for their gaze remains mobile. The general impression is dominated by a feeling of lightness, of the fluid relation between pieces, bestowing genuine unity on the exhibition experience.

In an article published in an important anthology, *Art of Projection* (2009), Mieke Bal analyses the intense feeling of immersion experienced when reacting to a video installation, and the hypnotic power that this has, quite independently of its narrative thrust.[4] She emphasizes the similarity between these works and the workings of dream, when subjectivity is absorbed in the scene of the unconscious. In both cases, the subject finds itself at the centre of a visual structure freighted with emotions, moving in the image without directing it, approaching the status of an actor on stage. Psychoanalysis has demonstrated the value of the theatrical model as a way of thinking about the working of dreams, and Bal uses it here to help get a handle on the effect of video installations. When we enter a Claerbout exhibition, we do effectively experience the emotions she describes; the narrative meaning eludes us but the rhythm of the images grips us strongly, carrying us along in a powerfully oneiric progress. We perambulate the picture walls with a feeling that we are taking part in a representation that speaks primarily to the senses, in which the body is an essential support for the reception of the works. If the looped videos seem totally independent of the viewers, and do not seek to

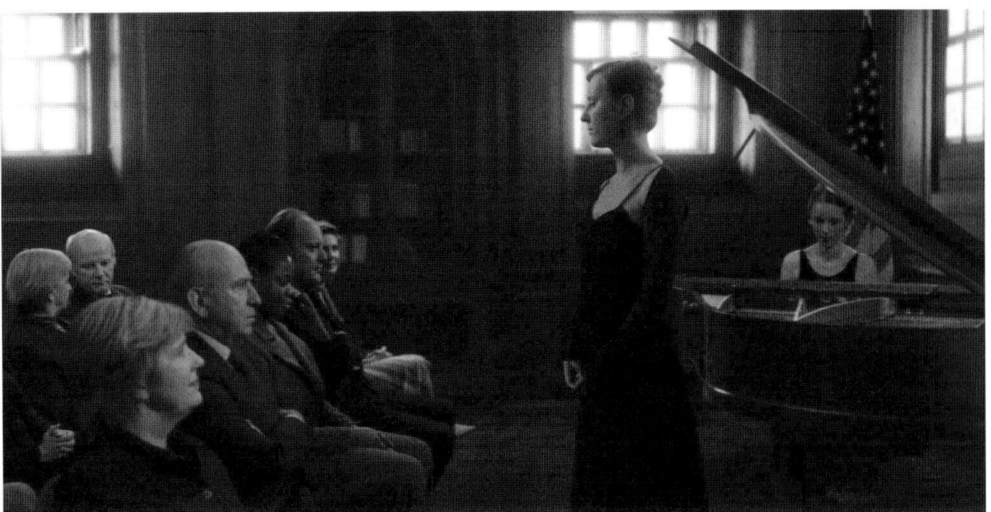

David Claerbout, *American Room*, 2009. Courtesy of the artist.

prompt their participation, viewers do need to be affectively receptive and to wander round the exhibition space for the artistic experience to crystallize on its stage. The imposing scale of the projections, closely related to the dimensions of the exhibition space, places the viewer in a frontal relation to an image that goes from floor to ceiling. The images invite them to mentally penetrate their spaces of representation, for example to join in the shadow of that old woman swaying gently back and forth in her *Rocking Chair* (2003), whose gaze occasionally meets their own. But this impression is only fleeting, and soon we are back outside the image. The handling of the exhibition space is not designed to include the beholder but to prompt a state of uncertainty in which they question their relation to the works.

With *The American Room* (2009), Claerbout extends this reflection on the stage space in another way, by focusing on a classical concert and the codes that structure its reception. Slow tracking shots show us an audience listening to an opera singer in religious silence. The recital is being given in an official venue: we see the American flag. The camera dwells on individual, concentrating faces, sometimes with a hint of a smile, their poses powerfully evoking bourgeois codes. The viewer is drawn into the emotion that seems to have brought all these people together, and this absorption is enhanced by the soundtrack and the visual rhythm. The singer is about to start *Amazing Grace*, a very popular Christian hymn. However, the music played by the pianist slowly fades before the concert can really start, so that silence gradually takes over again. The camera now moves around the auditorium, alternating between different viewpoints, allowing the gaze to dwell vaguely here and there. The music then strikes up again with the American national anthem, followed later by an Elton John song, all giving the scene a very conservative feel. A guard stationed at the entrance also seems captivated by the concert. The movement of the camera, the sound, the gentle light coming in through the windows and playing over the faces all confirm the theatrical dimension. But something important escapes the spectator here, upsetting them and preventing them from becoming fully immersed in the gathering. The particular relation between fixity and movement seems extremely problematic: as the camera eye peruses the scene, alternating between shot and reverse shot, the people here do not move. The video gives the illusion of taking place within a temporal density when in reality this is the frozen time of photography. Claerbout has a special penchant for this interplay between two regimes of the visible, but here it attains a new level in the deconstruction of our belief in the image. Each person was, in effect, filmed individually in a studio, then inlaid into the 'American Room', the trading room in an old London bank building. This actual gathering never happened. The actors never set foot in the room, and the concert, naturally, was never held there. Everything in Claerbout's video is false, reminding viewers of the constructed nature of their experiences.

In *The American Room*, Claerbout films what is a very old relation to the artwork—one that, like the people it shows, is very stiff. The reception of a work at a classical concert is governed by specific codes, established from defined places, in a framework that is not only closed but also, as here, surveilled. Everything soon seems false, not only the concert itself, but also the postures, the gazes, the expressions of concentration: each person seems, above all, to be putting on a show of listening. The hairdos are impeccable: the studied expressions

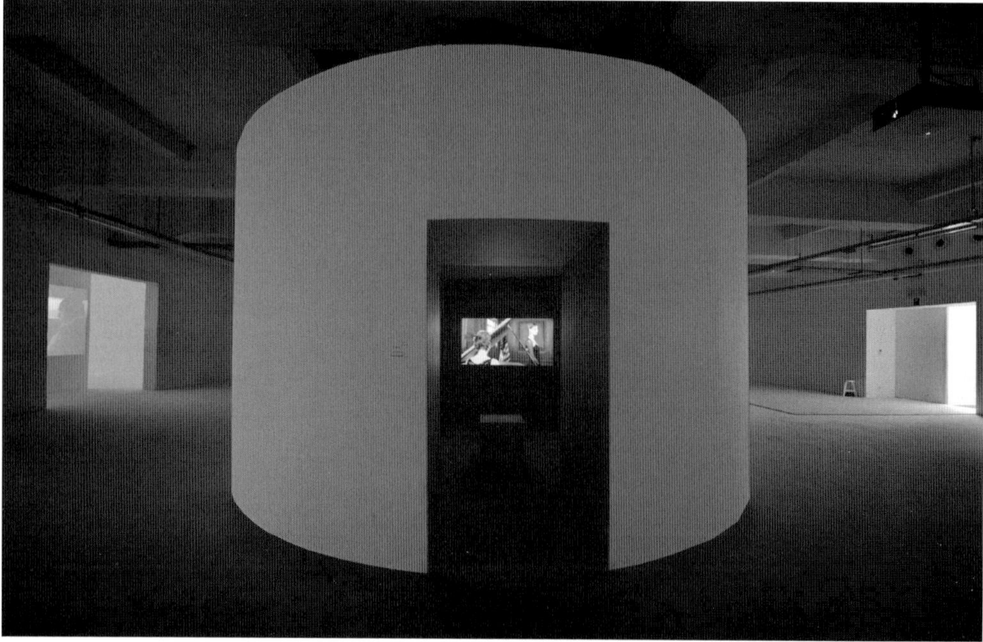

David Claerbout, *American Room*, 2009. Installation view at Wiels, Brussels, 2011. Courtesy of the artist.

give an impression of self-satisfaction. The faces have a knowing air that suggests class consciousness – a feeling of cultural superiority. The concert comes across more as a social event than as an authentic pleasure. The piece designates a performative register that seems at first sight more authentic than the one offered by the photographic medium, as a sharing of a given space–time, but here emptied of its substance, so that only the codes remain. Claerbout plays on the sacralization of the performative experience, of the art of the present, and catches the viewer in the trap of their own fascination with the concert form.

Video, as a multiple, affords viewers a moment of solitary reception; the organisation of the artistic event does not imply inclusion in a group. They come and go as they want, choose the moment and duration of their watching, without taking into account other people's listening patterns. This modality means an avoidance of closed receptive codes. Each piece can offer its own relation to the viewer, accepting its repetitive nature while offering conditions of reception that encourage the development of an individual perception of the work. When *The American Room* was exhibited at the Wiels centre in Brussels, in 2011, Claerbout placed it within a fairly narrow, spherical projection area soundproofed by acoustic foam. In contrast to the extensive area in which the other installations were placed, this set-up required that viewers isolate themselves in a mental space. By showing the foam covering the walls, Claerbout made evident the artificiality of the isolation, and the sense of confinement was further emphasized by the spherical structure. All these modes of presentation indicated a type of relation to the image that all Claerbout's work rejects. In this instance, it served simply to stigmatize the spectators represented in *The American Room*.

In comparison to this moment of collective sharing, which evaporates to leave only caricature expressions that are manifestly acted (faked), the other video works installed here seemed to offer the viewer experiences that were more imaginatively stimulating. The half-darkness imposed by the projection limits the impact of separation from other people's gaze, while the temporal openness allows each spectator to determine the duration of their immersion. Instead of staying in a given pose or place, the video installation effects a critique of certain traditional, rigidified forms of theatricality, which it makes it possible to escape.

The Movement of Gazes, Hesitancy of Bodies: Julian Rosefeldt and Ugo Rondinone

At the heart of installation is the concern to heighten the visitor's sensation of presence in a space and awareness of what is around them, to immerse them fully, not only as a viewer but also taking into account their corporeal nature. An installation is experienced with all the organs of sensation, not only sight but also smell, touch and hearing. Through a total physical experience, it opens up another register of aesthetic emotions, inscribing the relation to the work within the sensorial realm, introducing the visitor into another kind of relation to the world. The video installation calls into question the viewer's traditional reference points with regard to the work by immersing them in darkness, forcing them to grope forward, or to move while under the fascination of its moving images. The body must adapt to an environment in which sight and hearing are modified. It must enter into a truly performative experience that demands physical and mental commitment. The viewer is in a state of hesitancy. This is particularly the case when experiencing the works of Julian Rosefeldt and Ugo Rondinone.

Julian Rosefeldt: Movement and Compulsion

Shot mainly in 16 mm, the work of German artist Julian Rosefeldt (born 1965) is not only strongly influenced by cinema, but also explores the architectural spaces where it is exhibited. Seeing *Asylum* (2001–2, 52'), shown at the Hôtel-Dieu in Toulouse during the 2006 Printemps de Septembre festival, one was struck by the religiosity of the set-up. In a staging banishing any hint of realism, Rosefeldt placed nine screens around a large room.

The images showed undocumented immigrants: Afghan women vacuuming in a field of cacti, say, or Taiwanese prostitutes in a room where antiques were stored. The rhythm was slow, the light low, the figures silent. By showing groups of immigrants acting out the stereotypes usually associated with them, Rosefeldt theatricalized the everyday conditions of these marginalized and stigmatized populations. Played by amateur actors, all immigrants, these figures repeated actions that became absurd in the context where they appeared: a field of cacti took the place of an office block, a botanical garden replaced a kitchen, with Asian men in white chef's hats waiting idly, playing distractedly with the packaging scattered over the floor. Each screen had its own rhythm, and the ensemble created a constant but unaggressive hum. Spectators went from one screen to another, held by these cycles devoid of narrative content, guided by the images' power of attraction and the power of the emotions in a dreamlike fluidity. At some point, however, the installation crystallized, when

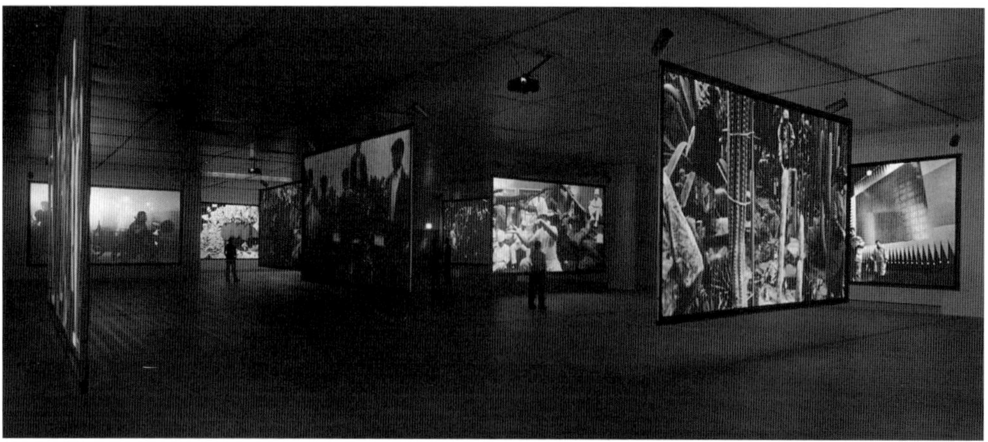

Julian Rosefeldt, *Asylum*, 2001/2002, 9 channel film installation. Installation view, Baltic Center for Contemporary Art, Gateshead, 2004. Courtesy of the artist and gallery Arndt & Partner.

the groups stopped what they were doing and began, one by one, to vocalize. This caused viewers to come to a halt, and turn around, struck by the magnitude of the choir taking shape before them. The great room at the Hôtel-Dieu echoed with their chants, expressing the humanity of the persons filmed, all gathering together to face the camera. Their role playing receded as a religious atmosphere came to the fore. In one corner, an old painting of Saint Vincent de Paul, patron saint of the institution, rescuing abandoned children from the street, had been left in its usual place. Given sufficient lighting by the projections to be part of the installation, it became the link between the street children of the Middle Ages and the homeless populations of the twenty-first century.

This installation is a fine example of the way in which a work can be reinforced by its context. The work existed before its Toulouse showing, yet one could not help feeling that it was being born for the first time in the Hôtel-Dieu. The religious nature of this setting naturally was conducive to a perception of the chorale as a moment of spiritual communion also including the spectator. The fascination created by the nine screens, capturing the gaze wherever it settled, was heightened by the multiple sources playing the song, filling the space and being further multiplied by the acoustic of the architecture. However, the immobilization of bodies, having them strike a religious pose that goes back millennia, was only temporal, and what followed were slow, unlikely scenes, with figures that were isolated or withdrawn into themselves. The visitor could once again move around among them. Compelled for a few moments by the power of the bodies gathered and united around them, visitors were all the more frustrated when returned to their solitary state, hesitating between two screens, between figures emptied of all personal expression.

In this work, Rosefeldt is exploring the ways in which a video installation can play with the viewer's body and emotions, manipulating them, compelling and then expelling them. While the work is certainly a plea on behalf of these marginalized and exploited populations, it also questions the spectacular registers that must be employed to elicit a response. What effects should be deployed to move, in spite of it all, a public that has grown used to the worst images of human injustice and violence? After experiencing the impact of the moment when the screens and actions synchronize, one realizes that there is a lot more to see and feel in the more evasive, more open and polyphonic effect of the narratives scattered around the space.

Trained as an architect, Rosefeldt is highly attentive to place, to the spaces he takes over, and reconfigures the rooms when the museum context is too neutral, thereby creating a genuine interdependence or play of resonance between the works and the setting. In 2010, his video, *The Shift* (2008), was thus presented at the Berlinische Galerie in relation to an older series, *The Unknown Cathedrals* (made in collaboration with Piero Steinle, 1995–97). The two sets of works were projected in rooms of the same size, linked by corridors with mirrors at the end, and separated by a room providing a kind of transition space that also showed an older work concerning Munich under the Nazis. The exhibition design helped shape the meaning of the work. The show as a whole thus played with the idea of a labyrinthine space, arousing sensations of déjà-vu with its mix of cinematic quotations, close filming of reality and revelation of a concealed history.

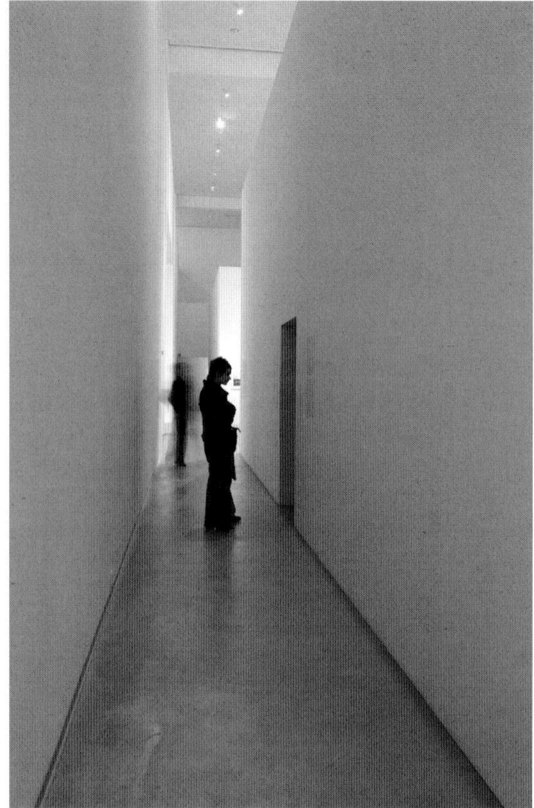

Julian Rosefeldt. Installation view, Berlinische Galerie, Berlin.
Courtesy of the artist and gallery Arndt & Partner.

In *The Shift*, Rosefeldt follows an actor performing the everyday life of four employees in a big electronic vehicle, a kind of craft strongly inspired by Stanley Kubrick's *2001: A Space Odyssey*. Only part of the sound in the installation came from this film and from *Solaris* by Andrei Tarkovsky, but their echo from the collective memory made these references much more intensely present. The man is completely isolated in a vast machine, which he moves through in long forward travelling shots, advancing down corridors, tunnels and spaces that are uniform and seemingly endless. The sound of his steps is the only element added to the muted electronic background, creating a highly austere world. The images are projected on four screens and the effect is almost hypnotic. The four images also echo the four roles played by the actor: scientist, night watchman, worker and maintenance worker.

Sometimes different roles collapse into each other, their combination presenting the different facets of a technological society where identities merge. The man performs his various tasks, like a tiny cog whose 'score', taken on its own, seems quite absurd: lowering the

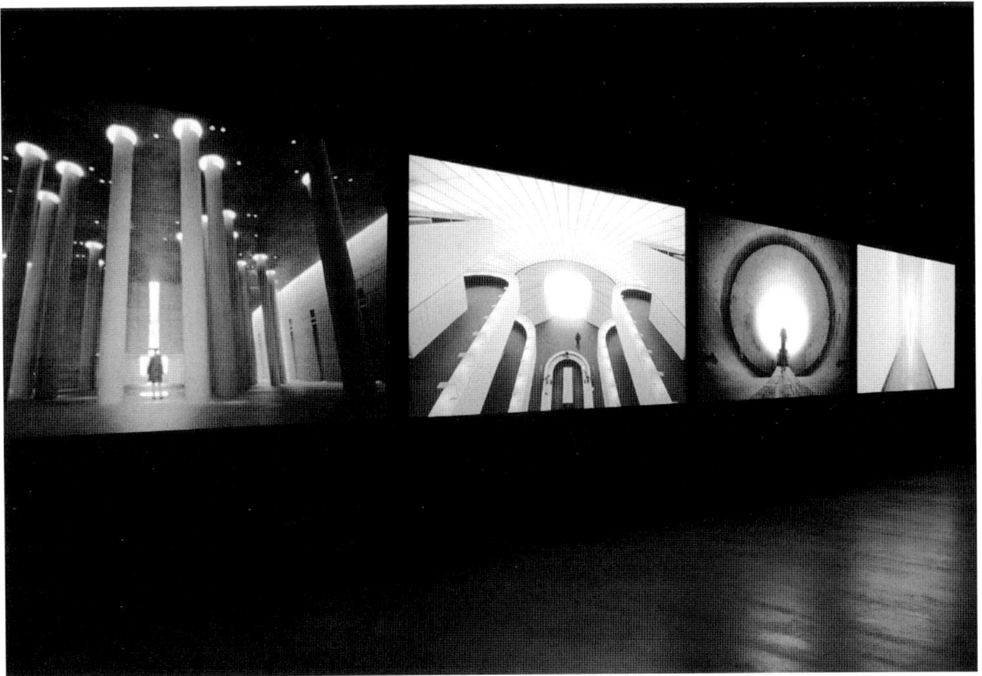

Julian Rosefeldt, *The Shift*, 2008. Installation view, Berlinische Galerie, Berlin. Courtesy of the artist and gallery Arndt & Partner.

seats in the rows of a huge auditorium, opening the drawers of a room lined with archives—his actions seem inept in comparison to an electronic universe where human action has all but lost its meaning. It is when he takes a break in the office that his individuality reasserts itself. A half-eaten sandwich, coffee flowing into a cafetière—such are the kind of details that tell the banal story of a life, the life of an employee who is no longer so young, alone in a science-fiction world. As he gets out his tuba and plays, the four screens concentrate on the melancholy atmosphere conveyed by the contrast between the melody and the coldness of the control room. With this music and these actions, the man reveals something of his inner life, which exists outside the round of his tasks. He never speaks to us, expresses nothing, does not even allow us to detect the traces of boredom or tiredness or, in contrast, pleasure. He fades into the universe that contains his days, literally disappearing when the four screens melt into dazzling whiteness. We then have the oneiric vision of the man walking on his own in a great expanse of pristine snow, marked only by his footprints. The symbolic impact is obvious. Rosefeldt says that his character is 'a kind of postmodern figure [...] caught up in a system that has become fully independent and has not needed him for a long time'.[5]

In all his films, individuals are immersed in a state of psychic and social isolation, locked into repetitive, absurd gestures, evoking traumas linked to their inability to inhabit a space,

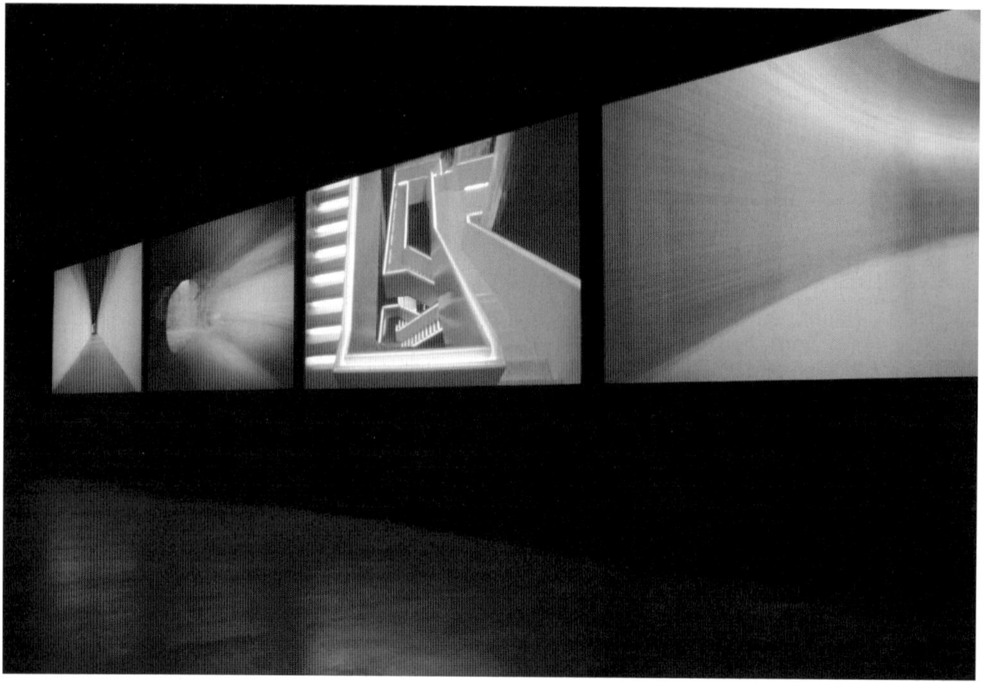

Julian Rosefeldt, *The Shift*, 2008. Installation view, Berlinische Galerie, Berlin. Courtesy of the artist and gallery Arndt & Partner.

to be part of a society that has lost its solidarity with its members. Through this installation, in which real places are treated as sets, Rosefeldt shows how our relation to the world has been emptied of its reality. Here, structures from the past (he films a scene in a tunnel that is at least a hundred years old) seem as artificial and unlikely as the ones created for science-fiction films. Whether shot in the studio or in real space, his images offer no clear indication as to their degree of authenticity. Every time, the filming techniques require a whole team of professionals, creating the conditions of this state of indeterminacy. There is thus a baroque dimension to Rosefeldt's work, deriving from the frequent mirror games and plays of illusion, often leading to a sense of dizziness and loss of bearings as to the status of what is being seen.[6] However, unlike baroque, the style he employs is extremely poised and simple. The sequences are long, the editing discreet, allowing full leeway to the actor's performance, giving them the time to exist within the place. Banal or meaningless actions nevertheless acquire great intensity in the existential solitude of characters deprived of speech. And still, we are unable to place them, incapable of saying whether they are fiction or even science fiction, or instead a reality perceived in all its theatricality.

Viewers entering Rosefeldt's exhibition at the Berlinische Galerie found themselves visiting their own history, like a kind of virtual avatar. The spectacular impact of the works cast doubt

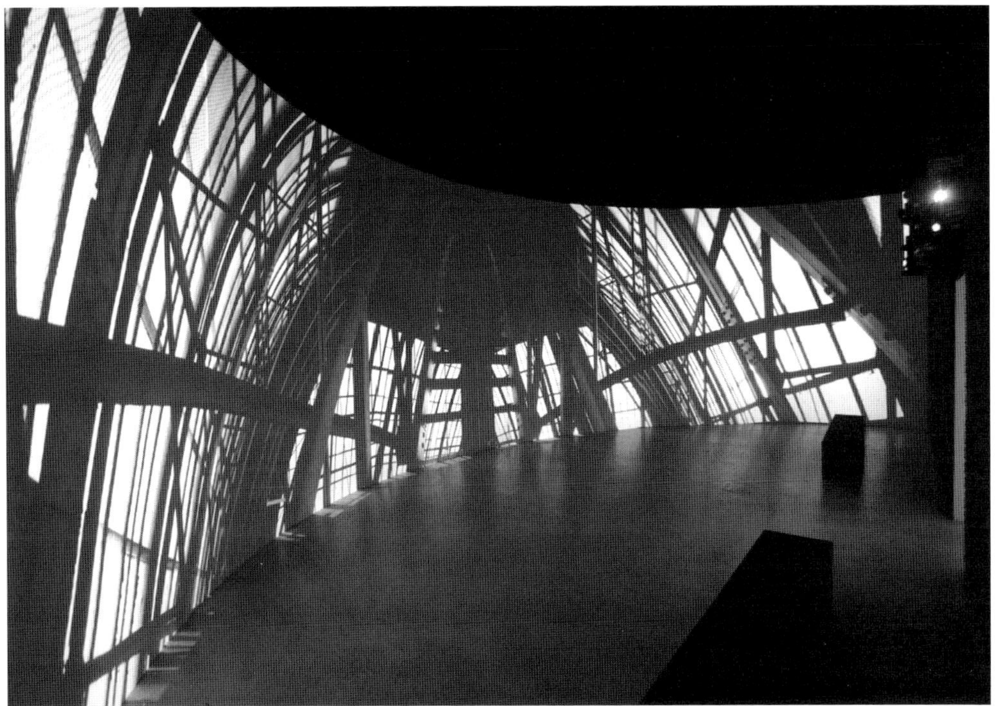

Julian Rosefeldt, *The Unknown Cathedrals* (in collaboration with Piero Steinle, 1995–97). Installation view, Berlinische Galerie, Berlin. Courtesy of the artist, Piero Steinle and gallery Arndt & Partner.

on the status of the beholder. If *The Shift* showed us spaces typical of our society (tunnels, control rooms) as fictional creations, the *Cathedrals* extend this state of confusion with immersive 180° views of these spectacular but ill-known structures. Rosefeldt went to places that are out of bounds to the public (like a waste treatment ditch) and to other more familiar places such as railway concourses and airports, and photographed them, in homage to the nineteenth-century tradition of panoramas, with a circular panning movement. This 180° view generates a new imaginary, flirting with the at once overwhelming and fascinating feeling of the sublime, offering us a non-human perspective on this architecture made by the human hand. The narrow corridor created in the exhibition at the Berlinische Galerie led us between this vision and that of *The Shift*, moving us joltingly between imaginaries where documentary and fictional perspectives intertwine. Between the two, the *Hidden City* (1994/2010) series presented a historical meditation on the interiorization of a past, between assimilation and negation, by looking at what has happened to the centres of Nazi power in Munich. The small format prints contrasted with the larger apparatus of the two other pieces, and this time the buildings did not pretend to be anything other than what they are. The play between their past and present states already raises sufficient questions about our relations to the architecture around us.

From one work to another, Rosefeldt questions our capacity to perceive our environment, to see what history, time and power hide from us. His stagings reference fictional universes so as to arouse curiosity about situations that are strongly inspired by the organization of our daily lives. Controlling the corporeal, visual and aural impact of his installations, he constructs temporal narratives that play on seductive effects (180° images, or the synchronization of images in *The Shift*, when the tuba sequence evokes the chorale in *Asylum*). These moments are part of a global experience in which Rosefeldt loses the spectator, leading them into dreamlike wanderings encouraged by the layout of the works in space. The loop in *The Shift* is evasive; the viewer is never really sure of having seen the complete piece. Impressions of déjà-vu come into play and it is impossible to tell whether images are re-appearing in another edit or if this really is the same projection as before. Viewers leave with uncertain steps, wondering if they should not stay a bit longer, and the play of mirrors in the exhibition set-up invites them to come back after having walked around, to inscribe their experience in the principle of the eternal recommencement that characterizes the actions of Rosefeldt's characters. A back and forth movement seems a necessity if we are to approach and experience a plural, non-linear and truly labyrinthine work. This quality is characteristic of many video works, in which the temporality of the narrative and the spatialization of the image produce a wavering reception.

Ugo Rondinone: The Walk of Bodies and Gazes

The mobility of a body in a space is what installed work seeks to create by means of specific presentation devices, and by playing on multiple screens, but also by treating movements as a subject. Filming walking creates a kind of redoubling that questions the spectator's relation to their experience of reception. Immobilized in their habits of looking, linked to the museum context, they are transported into a movement that leads them to the elsewhere promised by artistic creation. Rather than a window onto the world, the work is a path that vision alone cannot follow. It requires other senses, for as Marie-José Mondzain points out in *Homo Spectator* that vision is not limited to the organ of sight.[7] Being a spectator means having the courage to get onto the path of the work, of what surprises and transports us. Video installation speaks to the body, the better to remind us that in order to see we must commit ourselves, get moving.

Swiss artist Ugo Rondinone (born 1964) uses video in a body of work combining paintings, sculptures, photographs and drawings. He explores psychological states by creating hypnotic, melancholy installations. In *Roundelay*, shown in 2003 at the Pompidou Centre in Paris, Rondinone shows a man and woman walking through a city, over an ensemble of six screens. The projection apparatus creates a fragmented space that viewers are invited to enter. They must position themselves there and settle there. On encountering the work, from the outside, they are confronted with a structure that is formally simple and has sloping sides, interfering with spatial markers, and which they enter by a passage obstructed by bits of fabric. On entering, filaments of linen thus stick to the body, momentarily designating the physical engagement required by the act of reception. Christine Van Assche, the curator for new media at the Pompidou, described the architecture of the exhibition as 'an "unstable," truncated parallelepiped, close to the minimalist works of the 1960s and 70s', housing 'a hexagonal space hosting six projections'.[8] This description highlights the importance of the sculptural dimension in this video installation in which the exhibition space is conceived as a veritable extension of the image; not a simple set for the action, but a *mise-en-abyme* of the vibrations from the representation. A man and a woman, Joana Preiss and Gaston, are walking through the Parisian neighbourhood of Beaugrenelle, with its functional post-war buildings. Laid out over two levels, this neighbourhood was designed to combine housing, services and shops, thereby facilitating movement and avoiding confinement. Our experience of the area today, made perceptible in Rondinone's work, is the antithesis of that: the monotonous buildings are cold and featureless, the underground passages are austere and slightly sinister and the lines and chequering covering the floors and walls are thoroughly anonymous. An isolated individual walking through this neighbourhood is overcome with the sadness of this emotionally arid environment.

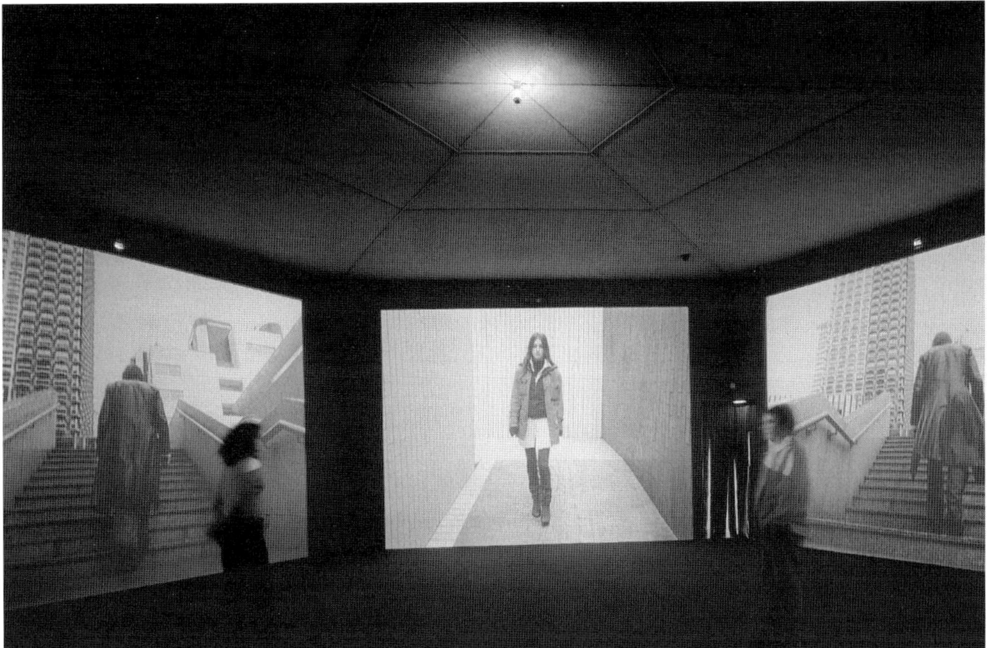

Ugo Rondinone, *Roundelay*, 2001–2002. Installation view, Pompidou Center, Paris, 2003. Photo: Jean-Claude Planchet. Courtesy of the artist and Pompidou Center.

The filming privileges close-ups on the actors' faces and feet, in a physical proximity that nevertheless remains fundamentally distant: no smile, gaze or expression breaks with the psychological remoteness. The image makes use of cinematic effects, such as the forward travelling shot, for their aesthetic impact, which softens the atmosphere. The night-time shots, with the lighted windows in the darkening sky, the fine rain, wetting the protagonists' hair and faces, help conjure up a poetic, melancholy vision of this Parisian stroll, which is broken only by a few dizzying impressions. When the edit accelerates—for example, when focusing on a given building—the gaze is effectively pulled in by what seems like a bottomless well. The music, an excerpt from *Islands* by Philip Glass (Glassworks, 1981), is minimalist and repetitive, combining and juxtaposing two strata, an arpeggio for violins and a melody for clarinet. Processed on a multitrack machine and spatialized, it constructs an enveloping ambience that monopolizes the attention, inviting viewers to respond with all their senses. They immerse themselves in a vision that leads them in a labyrinthine sequence that submerges them and engenders a feeling of plenitude. The movement of walking, the succession of long strides, nevertheless instils a vital energy and creates a tension, engendering the hope of an encounter that will not take place, except via the confrontation of screens.

A fusion takes place between the viewer and the images. This kind of installation creates total receptive experiences, in which the gaze cannot apprehend the work without

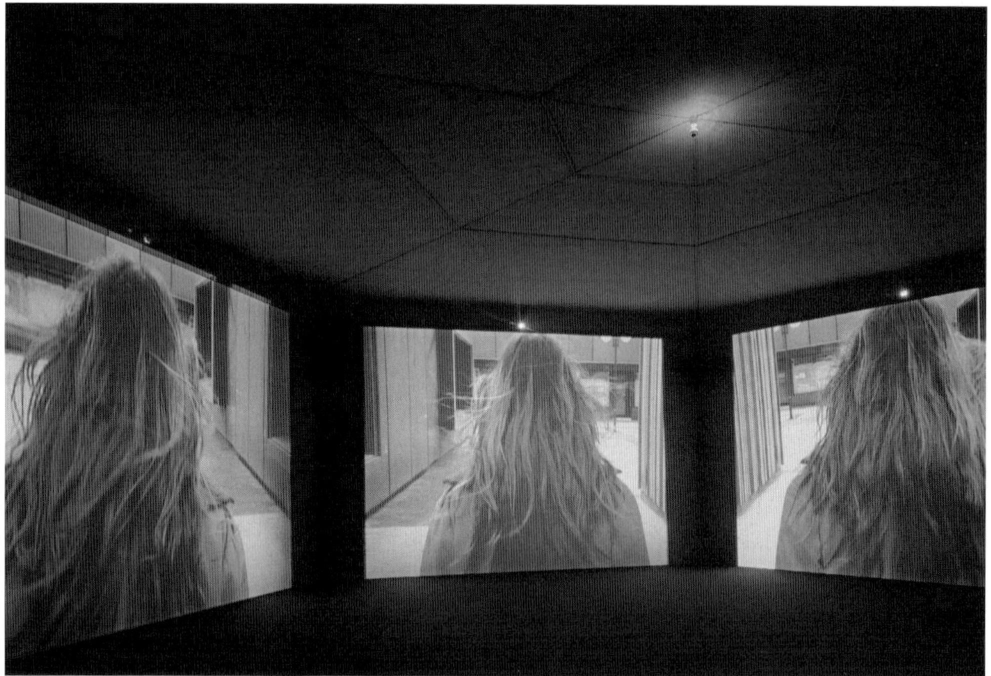

Ugo Rondinone, *Roundelay*, 2001–2002. Installation view, Pompidou Center, Paris, 2003. Photo: Jean-Claude Planchet. Courtesy of the artist and Pompidou Center.

combining with other organs of perception. The vision is rooted in the body, deploys and mixes with all the different sensations. The display set-up conceived by Rondinone for *Roundelay* reflects these concerns: in going from parallelepiped to hexagon, we go from a simple form to a complex one, figuring the transition from a rigorous, distanced register (the reference to minimalism is clear) to a subjective register, evoking the retinal fragmentation of the kaleidoscope. A few very fast successions of images in the edit, combining portraits and landscapes, thus create a powerfully sensuous stroboscopic effect. On entering the installation, viewers find themselves stuck and disoriented, unable to recognize the form projected on the outside from the inner volume. 'At the limits of the houseable, this strange apparatus, part sculpture, part penetrable object and architectural structure, seems to be pushing out the walls surrounding it and dumps visitors at the foot of its own walls'.[9] This description by Héloïse Lauraire suggests that the installation has an almost aggressive dimension, emphasizing its psychological impact. The images now take on a very different meaning; they loom up before us only after a destabilizing immersive passage, prolonging its effect by being projected on several screens. The forward movement of bodies in the urban landscape does not offer even the re-assuring guide of progression: spatial and temporal incoherence occurs frequently, strong light follows the dark night, until this returns again,

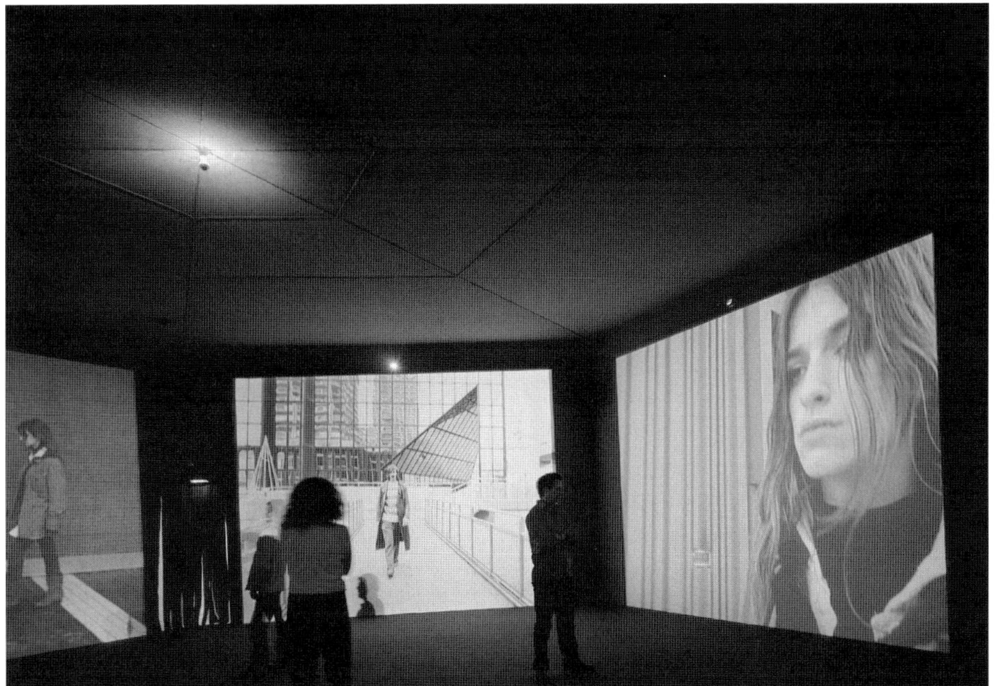

Ugo Rondinone, *Roundelay*, 2001–2002. Installation view, Pompidou Center, Paris, 2003. Photo: Jean-Claude Planchet. Courtesy of the artist and Pompidou Center.

and traces of rain suddenly disappear. Time always seems either too slow or too fast. As a result, the filmed scene loses its reality.

The melancholy atmosphere here is characteristic of Rondinone's work, in which dark doors are bolted, trees are dead and days are sucked into the infinity of constellations. Yet, a smile plays over the faces of the moon and the trees resonate with murmurs. The gaze feels disquiet as it enters this work made up of strange associations, unknown figures and equivocal impressions. As Gaby Hartel very appositely observes, 'Many of the facets of Rondinone's work can be properly apprehended only by the exercise of the gaze. Ambiguous, oscillating between the arts and lyrical prose, his work generally subverts our daily expectations. The uncertain ground is emblematic of this aesthetic of uncertainty'.[10]

The mobility of gazes is found in the swinging of the camera that picks out bodies, points up details and captures landscapes in its movement. We go from one composition to another without transition, and the editing is backed up by the rhythm of the soundtrack. Even when half-lying on the comfortable floor, viewers feel themselves being carried away in a meditative inner walk, where they can move around at will. In his dialogue with Doug Aitken, Rondinone explains the importance of the feeling of freedom that the installation offers the visitor, 'With a video installation, you can go in for a second, get the whole picture, and go out again. You can place yourself differently within the space as you walk through it. It's more like a dance than an inevitability. It's about using all your senses rather than only perceiving the moving image intellectually. […] It's an environment for the individual; there is a spiritual moment that it can give the viewer'.[11]

In an earlier installation by Rondinone there is a sentence that is repeated in a loop, *The evening passes like any other* (1998). It is echoed in *Roundelay*, 'What could be better, nothing is better'. Given the failure of our urban planning, despite all its genuine social ambitions, ours is no longer an age of revolutionary utopias but of withdrawal into subjective perambulations. The two figures each retreat into their privacy, into a mutual isolation that is all the more marked because they look like each other's double (their figures, the rhythm of their walking and the expressions on their faces all imperceptibly link them in a kind of mirror effect). The theatre of Samuel Beckett made a deep impression on Rondinone, and this influence is strongly manifested in this work, the title of which refers directly to a thirteen-line poem written by Beckett in 1976.[12] The characters do not talk, remaining withdrawn into the inner selves. Only their bodies give an idea of what is going on in their souls. Even if all this remains fairly vague, even if we do not really know what to think of this urban choreography, a familiarity develops. We let ourselves be swayed by the poetry of the walk, drawn by the turquoise of the man's shoes, contrasting with the dark colours of the winter clothes. This detail suddenly acquires a strange importance. Our vision deconstructed by the accumulation of screens, scrambled by the different tracks of the sound, spectators must find their own path. Discountenanced, they must agree to see differently, and also set out to explore the imaginary territories constructed by Ugo Rondinone.

Flight and Pursuit between Screens: Eija-Liisa Ahtila and Sebastian Diaz Morales

After walking, comes running, flight, the attempt to escape the field. The *mise-en-scène* of video screens allows a narrative construction that is particularly suited to a body in motion. Going from one screen to another, the figure questions his position in the filmic space and the spectator's relation to the frame of the image. In *Roundelay* the man and woman have a non-conflictual relationship to the environment that they are walking through, and make no attempt to abstract themselves from this environment, except via the reverie rooted in the experience of walking. They are, therefore, in an intimate, physical relation to the Beaugrenelle neighbourhood. In contrast, other works play on the multiplicity of screens in order to question the confinement of the body in a place, in the image, and in its attempts to escape. This problem is posed in installations where the space is intensively occupied, with videos juxtaposed and interconnecting, soliciting the gaze and constantly confronting it with its perceptual condition: its limited field of vision is incessantly faced with its incapacity to see, to grasp the diversity and the magnitude of the fictional space deployed by the installation. Seeking, nevertheless, to pursue the elusive work, viewers must constantly move their body and gaze, multiplying viewpoints and maintaining a visual vivacity in spite of the vertiginous impression that comes over them. This is the experience that we get from the videos of Eija-Liisa Ahtila, and that is at the centre of a work by Sebastian Diaz Morales, *The Man With the Bag* (2004).

Faced with fleeing figures looking for a gap in the fiction in order to get away from the real, spectators are torn between several images showing different, coexisting levels of reality. The break created by the splintering of the mono-screen implies a redistribution of places and roles. The viewer is positioned at the heart of the reception process by participating in its construction, while the artist's viewpoint becomes unstable and shifting. There are multiple cameras and because of the editing, it is no longer possible to unify perception and to establish bearings. It is the spectator's immersion (their progress through the fragmentation of the images) that provides the installed work with a constantly fugacious unity. Where one would expect the distancing affected by the elusive nature of the narrative to weaken the work, the distribution of the images, and the sound in space, in fact generates a very absorbing spectacular effect. Marcin Sobieszczanski puts his finger on this in his analysis of the cognitive questions raised by multi-screen works, 'The spectator's empathy with the Actors on the stage and with the Cameraman is created not only by the cinema effect, but at the same time by the effect of the spatio-temporal experience of the Spectator, to whom the spectacle is revealed as a result of their own action of sensorial orientation'.[13] Walking around the work becomes a real necessity here in order to recover the lost unity, and this makes the exhibition area a stage and place of movement. Flight, as we shall see in our analysis of the work of these two artists, then becomes a figure of displacement and mirrors the situation of the viewers themselves. Their fascination and their perplexity, their desire for both immersion and escape, the dominance of the psychoanalytical idea of the unconscious in their perception of the images, are all among the elements of analysis that we find in the construction of the works themselves.

Escaping the Real: Eija-Liisa Ahtila

Since the early 1990s, the video work made by Eija-Liisa Ahtila (Finland, 1959) has been centred on the exploration of psychological states. Her narratives owe a great deal to cinema, notably the quality of the images and the direction of the actors. However, her use of montage and multiple screens, and the fragmentation of the narrative construction over time and space, mixing the registers of documentary, fiction and fantasy, endow her work with a specificity that has made her a leading exponent of video art. Her works explore the relations between men and women and the question of femininity and offer real drifts into psychic intimacy. The figures she presents show the harshness and fragility of human relations, exhibiting repressed feelings and expressing the violence of emotions. Dialogue recedes in favour of the monologue that grounds the narrative in each person's confrontation with themselves, with their desires and with their cruelty. The images generally are attractive, for Ahtila accords great importance to landscape, light and the introspective poetry of the experience of nature. Sunsets over lakes, journeys through forests and isolated wooden houses constitute favoured backdrops for rooting the gaze in an exploration of the intimate and surprising it with the wounds it reveals.

While Ahtila's early works concentrate on Finland, her more recent film narratives go back and forth between different territories, not in an attempt to be eccentric but evoke the relations with elsewhere that we weaved and maintained in the past. *Where Is Where?* (2008, 58') addresses the theme of colonialism, exploring individual and collective memory from the starting point of an actual event. In the late 1950s, two young Algerian boys, excited by the violent atmosphere surrounding the beginnings of the war of independence, killed one of their French playmates. Franz Fanon commented on this tragic episode in *The Wretched of the Earth* (1961) and later published an interview with the two boys made as part of their psychiatric treatment. Ahtila takes the publication as her starting point, constructing a *mise-en-scène* that aims to both reconstitute the historical episode and confront it with the present of the narrative. A parallel narrative grows up around the daily life of a Finnish poetess who is also trying to express this history by reflecting on religion and guilt. This narrative duality sets up a relation between two countries and two cultures whose relations remain conflictual, and raises the question of memory and its transmission.

The six screens installed in the space offer several points of view on fiction and thus multiply the divided construction of the story. While the first one is used for the prologue and the last one for the epilogue, the four central screens facing inwards are where the story develops. Spectators must follow the images with their eyes, make choices and take part in the editing process. This splintering of the film is what enables Ahtila to have the different levels of the fiction interpenetrate, showing the Finnish poetess to be the author of the script, by the effect of strata, and gradually bringing the two stories together, until the incredible scene where the Algerians, now being chased, hide in the author's house, where they are finally discovered, woken up and killed. In this key scene, the figures flee a reality and at the same time exit the screen, and the change of frame also takes them onto another level of fiction, that of representation. The staging of the chase, from one screen to another, is a way of evoking the flight/chase between different levels of the real. An Algerian family runs away by stepping over the frame of the image, taking refuge in an area that is spatially and temporally out of the frame, ending up in the daily life of the poetess who, by her work of memory, brings the story back to life. Men, women and children are asleep on their feet, and now doze off in the Finnish living room. If sleep seems unlikely in such a situation, it references psychological reactions to the flight from reality. Unfortunately, the assailants, too, manage to find their way through the time of the narrative, and to perpetrate the avenging massacre.

This attempt to escape into another order of reality underscores the conflictual dimension of the relation to memory that, by evoking the injustices of human history, immerses us in a tragic moment from the past. The Finnish poetess is herself haunted by this obsession, by a guilt that pursues her and that she tries to propitiate by writing about history. Death enters the scene in personified form right at the beginning, and intervenes regularly in her quotidian experience, forcing her into intense and highly theatrical confrontations. This guilt is also rooted in religious spirituality. The installation title emphasizes a loss of spatial bearings: we no longer know 'what is where'; neither where we are nor where we're at. While watching this piece, we are immersed in a confusion of spaces and temporalities, between present and past, which raises the question of historical memory and of the reality in which each person stands. The construction of the installation, immersing viewers in darkness and imposing a constant need to move their body in order to follow the narrative, further extends this reflection. Viewers, too, must set off to discover the story in the film, and the path of reception is necessarily deceptive because they must allow themselves to lose their thread, to not see what they should have seen, to continue the story while choosing the framework of their own vision. They must enter into the construction of the narrative, a process that is at the heart of Ahtila's work, 'My interest has always been in the more abstract side of how to tell the story, instead of just in the story itself'.[14] The staging apparatus thus partakes of a reflection on the nature of narration that, while solidly grounded in text and in the work of the word, engages the spectator's body and perceptions. The visual impact of the images and the enigmatic quality of certain scenes captivate the attention and generate a certain disquiet.

Between the Screens: Sebastian Diaz Morales

The *mise-en-scène* that fragments a chase across several screens is also found in the work of Sebastian Diaz Morales (Argentina, 1975), whose essentially cinematic work constructs imaginaries on experiences of immersion in settings that may be natural, urban and human. *The Man With the Bag* (2004) is a strange chase through the wastes of Patagonia, constructed around a split screen, juxtaposing two points of view that convey the physical experience of the chase, but also helps create a new narrative framework. The scenographic device is much less complex than in Ahtila's installation; it consists of only two screens side by side and, what is more, the spectator is seated comfortably facing the image, in a frontal position closer to the cinematic model. The screen facing them is wider than usual, although its interest goes beyond the matter of size. It is not a panoramic screen, simply a divided double screen, and this division plays a key role. The action of the film, a man on the run, is built around this double space, and the narrative is sustained by what both links and separates the two images.

Throughout the film, the man tries to get away by going from one screen to another. The place of transition, the join between the screens, seems almost magical, a bit like the mirror in *Alice in Wonderland* by Lewis Carroll (1865), but also *Sherlock Junior* by Buster Keaton (1924), when Keaton walks into the screen during the projection. But then, in those two films, the subject is this relation between inside and outside: we are either in reality, or in a dream or fiction, and the protagonists' bodies enter into the mirror or the screen. In this case, in contrast, the man is constantly slipping from one screen to another, in a process that has now become something of a classic in video installations but is used to particularly meaningful effect here. The flight is orchestrated by the interplay between the screens. The man is trying to escape, to find the door that would enable him to slip out of the frame, to get out of the space of the chase. But in fact, this separation of the screens is not really that because they are stuck together and open no doors. The chase takes place on both screens, and there is no hidden exit in the space between them. Diaz Morales speaks of this dividing line as a 'boundary' or 'gap'[15] but in fact, what we have here is the impossibility of changing space, a non-frontier.

When multiple screens are used, usually it is because the artist wants to offer multiple viewpoints on a given story, and on a given space–time. Ahtila, as we have seen, excels at this practice; her films are constructed through the dialogue between screens, allowing us to grasp differing aspects of a given situation, to take a position that plays on an ideal omniscience. The gaze goes from one screen to another as it tries to follow the narrative in a purported visual exhaustiveness, serving a desire of total narration. The Moralez piece stands apart from this kind of practice, because two screens are relatively modest, and far from the monumentality of Ahtila's installation, or from Christian Marclay's *Video Quartet* (14', 2002), comprising a spectacular wall-like screen ten metres long.[16]

Compared to these spectacular installations, *The Man with The Bag* comes across as very simple. Diaz Morales organizes his dialogue between two screens because the basic reality of flight is the attempt to go from one space to another: to escape—to get out of the frame, to get out of a territory where we are trapped. The line between the two screens is the place where the attempt to escape from the chase is decided and where the actor and the spectator come up against the impossibility of getting away. Diaz Morales says that the line represents another obstacle for the spectator, poses a problem for their desire to watch the image and

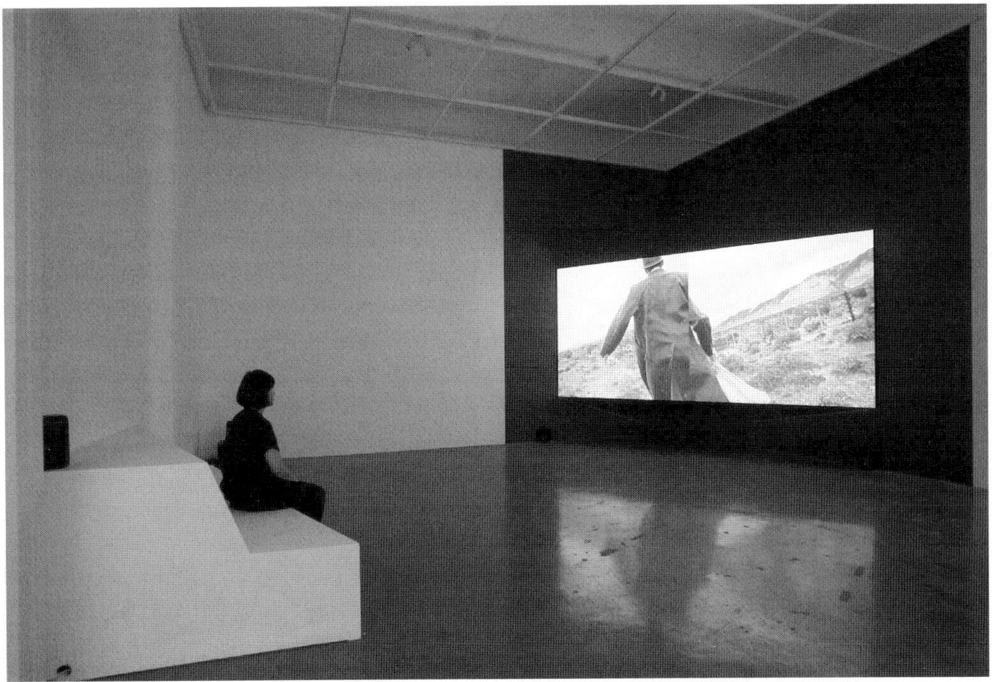

Sebastian Diaz Morales, *The Man with the Bag*, 2004. Installation view in 'Dans la nuit des images', Grand Palais, Paris. Courtesy of the artist and gallery carlier | gebauer, Berlin, gallery Catherine Bastide, Brussels.

the film. Separation is omnipresent, invasive for the gaze, it monopolizes the attention, we struggle to tear ourselves away from it. Spectators are trapped by this line that prevents them from settling into the image, just as it prevents the actor from escaping from the place of the pursuit. When he leaves the frame, he finds himself caught in another.

The double screen leads the spectator back to the experience of the duality of vision. They lose their unity of optical vision and are constantly reminded of the bi-partition of the gaze. Not only does Diaz Morales challenge the spectator's body, he also disrupts the unity of the filmed body, which is torn between two images, divided and stuck back together in a way that is often incoherent and inharmonious, by this dividing line between the two screens. The images often cohabit in a contradictory way (there are discrepancies in the colour), opening up a gap within the spatio-temporality. The body is central, because it is what imparts the rhythm to the movement forward in the landscape, what constructs the composition, but it is also a body as image. Like the landscape, which is redoubled and deconstructed, and in a sense dehumanized, an effect heightened by the absence of speech. In fact, the man makes no sounds at all, except for the cries of rage and exhaustion in the fifth episode. His inner feelings are sometimes made suddenly evident by his wild backward stare, but generally, his presence is distanced and aestheticized. His face is even overexposed, making his eyebrows an immaterial white. The man is voided of his identity. He is essentially a running body, a walking body, a divided body.

The rhythm of the chase alternates between moments of precipitation, when the man crosses the landscape, when he is putting all his energy into running, and moments of walking, when time seems to dilate and the chase to be suspended. There are lulls in the time of flight when the man busies himself with his bag and its strange contents, or simply observes the space he is travelling through. These are not really pauses because he continues to walk, but the imperative of flight seems to be suspended, leading to the idea that the pursuers exist only in the mind. In addition, while we sometimes hear barking, which can be worryingly loud, there is no actual sight of dogs, either. The man seems to have the power to keep them at a distance when his mind wanders, as when his attention turns to his shoe, which is caught in a rail. The wind turbines also point towards this idea of an imaginary, paranoid chase, in that they immediately bring to mind Don Quixote and his windmills. This is a man running away from his fears. When he calms down, when his anxieties recede, the barking fades away and the walk becomes calmer. The transitions from running away and moments of calm are abrupt and unpredictable, evoking the psychic mechanisms of anxiety. At what moment are we running away? When do we leave this state? How are the pursuers put at a distance? Such are the questions that arise here from a clinical viewpoint.

The image is regularly produced by a point-of-view camera that is guided by the movements of the body and thus constructs an immersive perception of the states of pursuit and drift. The noise of the footsteps is central. The camera pitches with the body and stumbles with the body. The landscape, too, is important: dry, desert-like, and grandiose, and the desire to convey its scale is another reason why Diaz Morales chose a double screen. The artist was born and grew up in the region and is strongly attached to it. It was therefore natural for

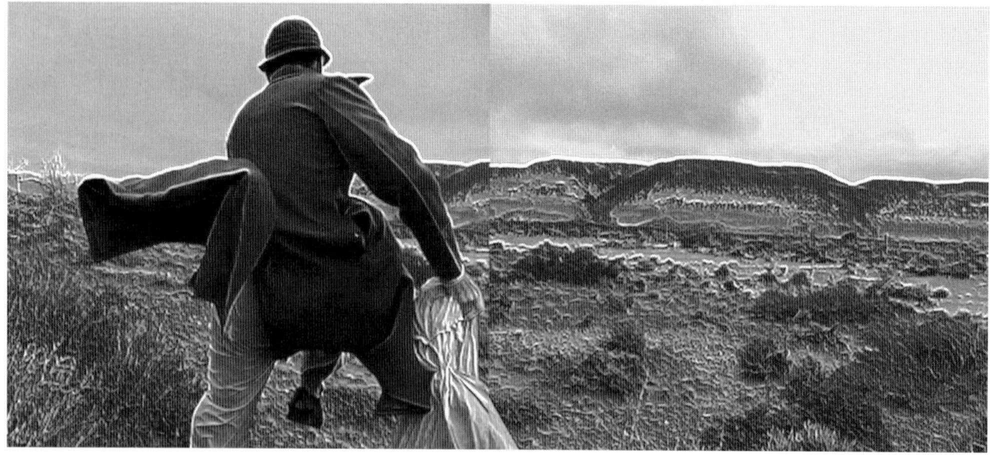

Sebastian Diaz Morales, *The Man with the Bag*, 2004. Courtesy of the artist and gallery carlier | gebauer, Berlin, gallery Catherine Bastide, Brussels.

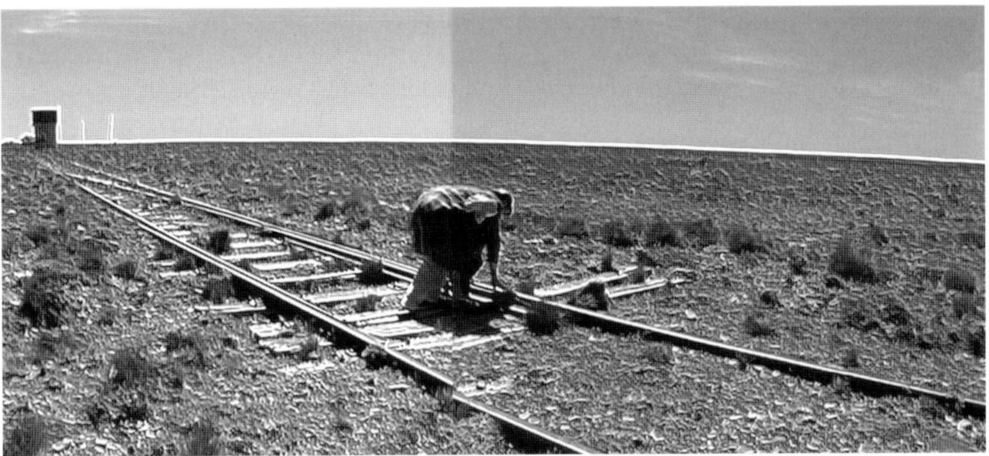

Sebastian Diaz Morales, *The Man with the Bag*, 2004. Courtesy of the artist and gallery carlier | gebauer, Berlin, gallery Catherine Bastide, Brussels.

him to come back and film it and help create a mythology for what is a relatively recently established population (the first villages were built 150 years ago). Diaz Morales emphasizes the land/sky boundary by outlining the horizon. His use of inlay effects brings to mind the universe of Thierry Kuntzel, who is concerned with the appearance and disappearance of the figure in space, and of the body in a landscape. In *The Man with The Bag*, the outlining also serves to link the two images, and offers a counterweight to the boundary created by the difference of colour, by skipping camera movements. Aesthetically, this line recalls the beginnings of video, electronic experiments and the walks of Ed Emshwiller, an American artist who, in *Crossing And Meetings* (1974, 30'), a film of a walking man, multiplied the figure and inlaid it in a variety of surprising surfaces. Here, the image is manipulated and creates a sense of unreality, emphasizing the oneiric dimension of the chase. The man's walk, his run, is regularly obstructed, as when a stone, a rail, or barbed wire gets in his way. At such moments, the landscape re-affirms its materiality, which is generally elided by the juxtaposition and manipulation of the images. Although it is fairly open, the countryside is hard to cross: the body must deal with obstacles, pick itself back when it falls. All this is very symbolic. The body is constantly drawn to the ground, by the gravity that hinders its flight; that hampers it. The man becomes a body again and the landscape a terrestrial reality, with its own logic, including the ability to test the man's body by causing him to fall. We see the man's weakness, his fragility, and also his indecisiveness. His walk is not that of someone with their mind made up: he does not follow a defined path, and seems somewhat unfamiliar with the environment he is walking through.

Right up to the end of the film, we have no idea of the reasons for this chase, but we feel the anxiety caused by the barking, rather like the sensations inspired by the Francis Alÿs (point-of-view) video *El gringo*, (2003, 4'12). In this video of Alÿs, the viewer feels the anxiety of a man attacked by a pack of baying dogs, climaxing in the final scene when he drops the camera and the barking becomes unbearable. In *The Man with The Bag* when the barking gets closer, we feel assailed, but ultimately what is constructed is a chase in which the dichotomy of pursuer and pursued disintegrates as the two parts merge into a single entity, which is the man's psyche. The music plays a major role here by breaking up the long moments of silence and clearly lightens the drama of the ensemble. Composed by Simeon ten Holt (Netherlands, 1923–2012) in 1979, it comprises short sound sequences for two pianos that can be repeated an infinite number of times to create a hypnotic, obsessive but also rather light and soothing atmosphere. This distances the viewer from the man's emotions, preventing them from really entering into the narrative, and contributes to the overall impression of non-linearity. Unlike *Gerry* by Gus Van Sant (2002), which some of the scenes in *The Man With the Bag* reference, and in which viewers are caught up in a story, in a human experience of limits, here the construction plays on contradictions, suspense and absurdity, preventing us from entering into any kind of fiction. And unlike the protagonist in *Gerry*, the man here is trying to escape the baying of his pursuers but not the landscape. He seems at home in the austerity and solitude of the desert; he is not trying to leave them behind. When he comes to a railway, which ends in the middle of nowhere, he does not walk back along it to reach civilization, he crosses it and moves away. The ending precisely echoes *Gerry*, in that the man comes to a road and gets into a car, leaving his bag behind him. However, this is a false getaway because the car drives back to the start, where the man gets out, takes up his bag and strikes out again. The walk seems to have no end; the pursuit, the man's quest, remains open. It is a physical and mental ordeal lived in solitude. When he gets out of the car, the barking stops, but it will no doubt start again shortly afterwards and his running will continue. The division of the work into episodes gives the impression of a progress, an evolution. For example, we can tell in which episode the suitcase turns into a bag of bones. But ultimately, the division is there only to signal more emphatically the cyclical, endless dimension of the pursuit. This is reinforced by the installation set-up, in which no sooner does the film come to an end than it starts again—with a relentlessness reminiscent of Beckett's plays, with which this video resonates in more ways than one.

The split screen thus allows a narrative that contains a discrepancy, playing on numerous resemblances with cinema while also distancing itself from it, installing a practice of the image in which the double frame structures the film narrative, enclosing it in the tension of its scission. Without words, with great narrative economy (almost nothing happens), this video typifies the way in which a work can be built around a particular apparatus.

Notes

1 El Lissitzky, quoted by Yve-Alain Bois, 'Exposition : esthétique de la distraction, espace de démonstration', *Cahiers du Mnam* no. 29, p. 72. English translation in Bruce W. Ferguson, Reesa Greenberg, Sandy Nairnes (eds.), *Thinking about Exhibitions*, Routledge, 1996.

2   Françoise Parfait, 'L'installation en collection', in *Collection Nouveaux Médias. Installations*, Éd. du Centre Pompidou, 2006, p. 39.

3   Interview with Christine Van Assche, *David Claerbout, The Shape of Time*, JRP Ringier, 2008.

4   Mieke Bal, 'Setting the Stage: the Subject Mise En Scène', in Stan Douglas and Christopher Eamon (eds.), *Art of Projection*, Hatje Cantz, 2009, p. 167–81.

5   *Living in Oblivion*, discussion avec Guido Fassbender and Heinz Stahlhut, Kerber Art, 2010, p. 37.

6   On this point, see Stephan Berg's essay in 'Play It Again' in *Julian Rosefeldt Film Works*, Hatje Cantz, 2008.

7   Marie-José Mondzain, *Homo Spectator*, Paris: Bayard, 2007.

8   Christine Van Assche, 'Roundelay, de Beaugrenelle à Beaubourg', brochure for the exhibiton of Rondinone's *Roundelay* at the Pompidou Centre from 5 March to 28 April 2003, Paris: Éd. Centre Pompidou, 2003.

9   Héloïse Lauraire, 'Ugo Rondinone, Roundelay', www.mouvement.net. Accessed 12 March 2003.

10   'En s'adonnant à l'illusion…', Gaby Hartel, brochure for the exhibiton of Rondinone's *Roundelay* at the Pompidou Centre, op. cit.

11   *Broken Screen. 26 Conversations with Doug Aitken*, Ed. d.a.p., 2006, p. 238.

12   See 'En s'adonnant à l'illusion…', Gaby Hartel, op. cit.

13   Marcin Sobieszczanski, 'Une théorie génétique de la monstration vidéofilmique distribuée spatio-temporellement', in Peter Lang (ed.), *From Split-Screen to Multi-Screen. Spatially Distributed Video-cinematic Narration*, Bern, 2010.

14   Eija-Liisa Ahtila speaking to Doris Krystof in *Ahtila*, K21 Hatje Cantz, 2008 p. 179.

15   Discussion with Geert-Jan Strengholt published on www.sebastiandiazmorales.com.

16   This piece was exhibited in *Christian Marclay: Replay* at the Cité de la Musique, Paris, 2005.

Chapter 2

'Inhabiting the Scene'

When Video Engages with the Theatrical Model

Video art is often defined by its critical proximity to television and cinema. While these connections are certainly essential, and especially the ones with cinema, whose narrative codes are explored and displaced by artists, as we have seen in the work of Sebastian Diaz Morales, not enough is made of the importance of video's relation to theatre. Many works offer a vision of the world embraced by the stage, re-appropriating the history of theatre, acting and actors, and theatrical architecture. Different kinds of stages, from theatrical ones to everyday places, are occupied in these fictional constructions that interrogate the way in which a body can inhabit a set. The question of acting and embodying a role is also at the heart of works offering a meditation on the frameworks of theatrical experience.

The Loss of the Character: James Coleman, Maïder Fortuné, Michael Snow

The twentieth century was a time of crisis for the theatrical character, who was a victim of the calling into question of drama. History was gradually expelled from the stage, sometimes in very radical forms. The German critic Hans-Thies Lehmann described this theatre as 'postdramatic' and argued that in its plays 'the progression of a story with its internal logic no longer forms the centre'.[1] The temporal and spatial markers of drama gradually disappeared. The narrative substrate became increasingly slim, mythological references disappeared, leaving the spectator not only at a loss but also, very often, deeply touched by the existential quest and by the great universal questions expressed in contemporary theatre. The character became a figure voided of its substance, a silhouette played by the body of an actor, an echo of the crisis of values, beliefs and identities that pervaded the last century and continues today.

This situation has been summed up as follows by Jean-Pierre Ryngaert and Julie Sermon, 'The contemporary character is marked by the present, is often without a past and has no projects, no trajectory. Sometimes he dwells permanently in a present of reiteration: the past immobilises him. He knows his ellipses, he proceeds by temporal leaps and fleeting moments'.[2] Many artists show an interest in theatrical characters and feature them in videos that probe this crisis. In these works, as on the stage, the characters have unstable, problematic, disconcerting identities, and what we see on-screen extends the upheavals that have occurred on stage since the start of the twentieth century. Beckett's influence is particularly strong, as mentioned above, and is often evident in videos representing the vicissitudes of the human condition. The discourse on contemporary theatre has increasingly substituted the term 'figure' for that of character, reflecting this evolution towards more evanescent identities. As it happens, the term itself is taken from the visual arts, and it is natural that video works should have appropriated it in turn, prolonging the mediation on the nature of stage performance from their own specific position.

Today, indeed, video is often conceived as a creative support for actors facing the character's loss of substance. As Jean-Louis Besson puts it in his introduction to the volume *L'acteur entre personnage et performance*, contemporary writing, the heir of 'postdramatic' theatre, finds that artistic transversality provides resources to deal with the emptiness left by the crisis of the character. Video, new technologies and artists' stage designs are increasingly prominent on stage, and 'the actor, whose traditional role it is to carry the text, is thus forced to face new challenges'.[3] The actor shares the stage with the projected image, with the screen, with his own doubles, in an evolution whose first experiments go back to the turn of the twentieth century and the work of Edward Gordon Craig and Vsevolod Meyerhold, as mentioned in the introduction.[4] The closeness of theatre and video no longer requires advocacy. Numerous directors work with a multiplicity of mediums and exploit the dramaturgical qualities of the filmed image. Moreover, this reterritorialization of video on the stage makes it possible to reveal a fundamental bond between the two mediums. The back and forth between the image and the stage denotes a creative richness generated at the confluence of theatrical and filmic questions, whether on stage or in the exhibition space. I wish to discuss this here through analyses of the work of three artists from two different generations: James Coleman, Maïder Fortuné and Michael Snow.

James Coleman

The question of theatricality is found throughout the work of James Coleman (Ireland, 1941), who uses sound, slides and video in pieces that question the construction of the image and identity. While the immersion of the viewer is central to his first works (as in *Installation Made for Location*, 1975), in which the viewer has a bodily involvement and experiences a loss of bearings, more recently Coleman's art has played with their desire for identification. He is interested in the projections and stereotypes that construct human relations, in the artefact of memory, and in the fictionalization of the past through the complex process of the emergence of memories (*Clara and Dario*, 1975). Drawing on personal narrative, popular culture, the media and history, his pieces put individuals at their centre, but there is a sense of unease about their identity, which is often unstable. Coleman's subjects are in crisis, have lost their unity and are struggling with their own disappearance. The video *Box (ahhareturnabout)*, 1977, is a portrait of Gene Tunney in his mythical fight against Jack Dempsey in 1927, when he was fighting to keep the title of world champion he had won the year before. With this identity at stake, the issues for Tunney were above all psychological and social. He had to put himself on the line in order to continue being what he was: a world champion. Coleman's highly realistic characters, filmed in an objectivist aesthetic, reveal the theatricality of the construction of human lives, the need to be constantly acting, inhabiting the real, unifying multiple identities in action so as to avoid dispersion.

Language is essential in this questioning of the subject, which partakes of a reflection on its narrative and fictional dimension. Monologues and dialogues create conflictual portraits in which intertwining stories have a complexity that directly reflects the analysis of the contemporary subject. The tone of voice is often highly personal, engaging the viewer in an intimate relation, but the process of projection is thwarted because the attraction generated by the character is paralleled by repulsion at their state of crisis, which makes them incomprehensible. The unease generated by Coleman's works is very much part of what they are about. The viewer's uncertainty and mystification are a response to a meditation on the workings of relations to the other. By showing figures who are torn, Coleman probes identities in crisis, and the viewer becomes involved in their striving through their own experience of unease. Jean Fischer has produced a subtle analysis of this reaction, '[…] in the face of the work's constant slipping away from any determinable referentiality, the viewer experiences a suspension of knowledge, a rendering "speechless," a loss of boundaries between subject and object. In other words, the work induces moments of desubjectivation, a state of uncertainty that can be referred neither to a subject nor to a psychological state'.[5] Without grasping everything they are seeing, viewers feel a fascination that involves them while keeping them at a distance.

Retake with Evidence (2007, 46') is an enigmatic work at the heart of these issues, in which we observe a performance by a real actor. Alone in a space with indefinite boundaries, Harvey Keitel moves slowly, his face full of anxious lucidity. In a Shakespearian language tormented by ancient tales, betrayals and the possibility of forgiveness, the aging actor, simply dressed, wanders over a stage, speaking to men in tones with a hint of tragedy. From time to time, a set appears—pasteboard buildings and Greek statues in cardboard sets. Coleman had long been concerned with theatricality and its conditions of appearance, but in this video, which is viewed from a large room closed off by a glass pane, he went a step further. The image of the actor's body is the place where language and theatre are experienced. The effect is stunning: we are compelled by the dramatic tension, even though it is difficult to grasp the narrative. The text seems to be a compilation of excerpts. Some have attributed them to Shakespeare and others to Aristotle, but they could just as well have come from the actor's memory. Coleman provides no keys, refuses to pair a text with his installation or to help visitors find their way around the experience. The pane of glass that divides the large, dark projection space allows the viewer to hang back, to see without becoming immersed in the representation. It provides them with the freedom to see the exhibited work and other spectators captivated by the monumental image, by the enigmatic narration. In his analysis of this work, Raymond Bellour emphasizes the existential quest acted out by Keitel, evoking 'This body of a suffering actor, a soul grieving for itself and for the world, these stuttering breaths, these sighs inlaid into the words, against the stage backdrop in a moiré blue-grey that, above all, strongly evokes those desolate seascapes by Gerhard Richter where sea and sky merge'.[6] The texts plunge the actor into an anxiety at the passing of time, giving the installation a tragic tone. And yet, no narrative really becomes established here because the monologues are isolated and shorn of context, and cannot be properly grasped. Some of the words resonate, however, and the viewer can focus on Keitel's facial expressions, or again, let their gaze slide over the strange sets brought from the basement of history. The quality of the actor's presence is as powerful as it is intriguing, and in this sense, strongly illustrative of the rupture of postdramatic theatre that, as Hans-Thies Lehmann points out, offered as the alternative to the model of representation 'the utopian ideal of "radicalised" presence'.[7]

Retake with Evidence echoes an older video, *So Different... and Yet* (1980). In an architectural setting that the artist changes every time it is exhibited, the work consists of a single television screen, backlit by a coloured light. In the background, a pianist (Roger Doyle, who composed and performed the music) talks in the third person, playing the role of the narrator. In the foreground, a contemporary odalisque (who could be a model), wearing a bright green dress and a red ribbon wrapped around her leg, becomes the visual focus of the work. The work suggests a certain kinship with *Center* by Vito Acconci (1971), in which the artist, like Coleman's woman, is positioned close to the camera and seems to want to communicate privately with the viewer. However, whereas Acconci speaks directly to the person facing him, encouraging them to come closer and giving an impression of physical proximity, the pianist's incomprehensible monologue loses the viewer. Like Acconci, Coleman is interested in our relations to the film or television image, and in the perceptual disruptions that they generate. *Center* and *So Different... and Yet* question the modalities of encounter in a virtual relation, oscillating between intimacy and isolation, both of them fantasies. Here, we are back with the question of theatricality and the attempt to break down the 'fourth wall' that traditionally separates actors from the audience and the auditorium. The separation induced by representation, by the spectacularization of the world, places the artist in a struggle with the same desire to call into question the distance between the image and the gaze. What is played out here in a reflection around the screen, around the glass pane, and what has been at the heart of video art from the start joins up here with the issues characteristic of the history of theatre, when directors and dramatists called into question the symbolic attribution separating spectators from actors. But what can be done in live action, which opens up new territories of performance, cannot be done in the same way in the video image.

That is why Coleman's work does not try to cancel this separation, but works instead to signify it, to stage it. In *So Different... and Yet* as in *Retake with Evidence*, the viewer is in an ambivalent position, drawn in by the seduction of the character, of the actor, but excluded by the impossibility of entering into the narrative. The glass that divides the space of *Retake with Evidence* clearly designates this uncomfortable position imposed by Coleman. The gaze can choose to cross it or go round it, but it cannot obliterate this screen surface that reminds us of the nature of projection itself. Despite the strong impression of the presence given by the actor, the scene is no more than an image. These two works are performances by actors and maintain the conditions of theatre. The actors clearly address the viewer with their emphatic, frontal gaze. We could be at the theatre. But what faces us is an image, whose regime of appearance is the repetition of a looped video. The image draws us in and leaves us out, the spectacle is constantly elusive. The *here and now* of theatre are invoked as illusory powers.

Maïder Fortuné

The recent work of Maïder Fortuné (France, 1973) connects with some of Coleman's concerns. Trained at the Lecoq theatre school in Paris and at Le Fresnoy, Fortuné uses mainly video but also photography, sculpture and performance. Her career has taken her from the stage to the exhibition space. This displacement is at the heart of several of her pieces, including the ones shown in *Whispering in Distant Chambers*, her 2008 show at the Martine Aboucaya gallery in Paris.

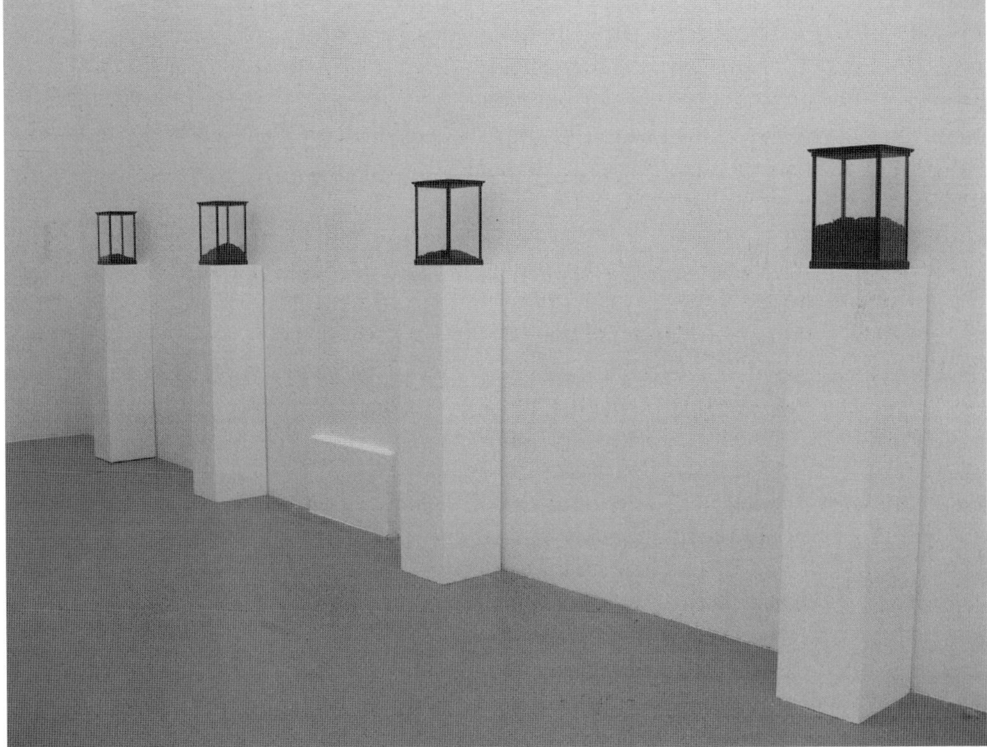

Maïder Fortuné, *Characters*, 2008. Courtesy of the artist.

Characters is a series of four sculptures, each one dedicated to a particular theatrical character: Hamlet, Antigone, Doctor Faustus and Salome. In individual glass boxes, small black enamelled letters form illegible piles. The gaze moves around, searching in vain for guidance, lost by the accumulation of letters and by the absence of words, as if surveying an enigmatic cemetery of language. In reality, the letters are not there by chance: they come from a text spoken by the corresponding figure on stage by the theatrical characters mentioned. They derive from selected theatrical speeches and dramatis personae. Enclosed in these little glass theatres, without the architecture supplied by text and the actors' bodies, these mythical roles lose their power and identity. In Fortuné's piece, we basically have no ways of distinguishing between Hamlet and Antigone, except perhaps for the differing heights of the piles, suggesting a comparison between the different textual densities embodying the characters. The titles designate the hiatus between these silent sculptures of the heroic figure evoked by the name. The character collapses when the text comes apart, calling into question a certain kind of theatrical form. The tragic hero caught up in a whirlwind of events, placed at the heart of a story, a complex and remarkable identity, is a figure that has been lost to contemporary representations. This piece by Fortuné evokes its disappearance, linked to the questioning of narrative identity emblematically exemplified by the theatre of Beckett. The figure is now lost in a splintered world with diffuse values, and unsettled, unable to get a grip. The title, *Characters*, designates this gradual shift in which the characters are voided of their substance and end up as nothing more than block letters. Fortuné brought boxes back from Japan, where they were used to display dolls. By replacing substitutes for the body with piles of letters, *Characters* evokes the distancing of the actor, of performance and of the character. These urns leave viewers alone with the emotions suggested by these piles, seeking to retrieve fragments of text from the depths of their memories.

Curtain!, a video shown in the same exhibition, extends this theme. In the dark, viewers watch a ghostly procession of fairy tale and comic book heroes, many in the form given them by Walt Disney. Batman, the Queen of Hearts, Snow White and many others back towards us, then disappear into a thick, dark fog. Dressed in black, they enter the image to the rhythms of a muted industrial soundtrack, in an oppressive, sinister atmosphere. Their tread is heavy, solemn for the Queen of Hearts, precious for Snow White. The installation set-up totally immerses visitors in the work, giving them the impression of walking with the characters on a kind of purgatorial journey. There is no glow of light to guide their steps or comfort souls. The only brightness comes from the sides and produces, rather, an effect of blindness. Isolated from their fictional universes, the heroes are evoked only by their attributes—mask, sceptre, hair, etc.—and the impression they give is above all of a lack of substance. Sometimes, these silhouettes shown from behind are impossible to identify—the faces are hidden. Cut off from their narrative contexts, they no longer project us into fantasy tales and instead show only these sad, dark forms. Fortuné deconstructs our image of these cartoon versions, showing them in an ultimate crossing of the screen, where their efforts to once again embody a role are no longer enough to re-awaken the dream. When the curtain is down, the magic fails. The

Maïder Fortuné, *Curtain!,* 2008. Colour, sound, 18'. Courtesy of the artist.

exclamation mark of the title references the energy that closes the time of the representation and evokes the atmosphere of a live show. In this video, the heroes are played by flesh and blood actors, but the vitality of acting has deserted the stage. A new kind of relation then develops with these odd, light figures that inhabit our memories: the loss of colour, the hesitancy we perceive in their movements and their oppressive silence designate the transition from the joyous cinema of childhood to the cold and empty theatre of everyday life. The procession taking place before us seems endless, and the loop heightens this impression by removing any kind of temporal marker. In its indefinite time and space, *Curtain!* offers a dreamlike spectacle in which shadows are the supports for our memory's projections.

This relation to childhood is a recurrent feature of Fortuné's work, whether she is playing a young girl evoking silent movies, photographing children or filming a unicorn. This imaginary enables her to bring out its singular emotional density. *Curtain!* combines the pleasure of reunion with key figures of the imagination and the sad disappointment of seeing them disappear into a colourless, storyless abyss. The absence of words intensifies the feeling of loss conveyed by this video, which also marks the end of a certain regime of embodiment. Without a role to project themselves into, without a stage to inhabit, the heroes wander in the dark corridors of fleeting reminiscences.

The exhibition title, *Whispering in distant chambers,* referred to an unshot script from 1966 by Jacques Tourneur, in which two men try to scientifically prove the existence, or non-existence, of ghosts. Fortuné, too, went in search of souls that wander in the density of our memories, and on stages bereft of stories. The sudden appearance of images is always unexpected, fragile and tenuous, and occurs in places deserted by the characters: where the film project stumbles, where the text finds no body to sustain it, where the imaginary has no substance left to nourish fleeting impressions. In these indeterminate zones, on the fringes of theatre and cinema, video questions the heritage of these arts of execution. It is a privileged locus for staging the loss of the character in contemporary theatre, for questioning the transition to a body that serves as an image without being inhabited by dramaturgical narrative. This reflection is also found in *A venir*, a set of four short videos shown on a single monitor, in which small dots of light represent motion capture, ready for future digital creations. Like Pierre Huyghe and Philippe Parreno with *Annlee*, Fortuné is interested here in what goes on behind the scenes in the modern digital theatre. The light codes of *À venir* are the stage that precedes virtual animations, in which, thanks to these armatures, the drawing can closely follow the movements of the human body. The viewer is confronted with a character in a hybrid state, without a face or a story, but with a visual structure.

The performative dimension was central in Maïder's first works, whose images showed bodies acting, struggling and moving. Its disappearance is thus all the more striking here, pointing us towards other modalities of presence. Faced with the misty silhouettes of *Curtain!*, with the theatres without actors of *Characters* and with the movements without substance of *À venir*, spectators are forced back to their own perception, to the temporality of their relation to the work. They are placed on stages deserted by the body but peopled with images and figures.

In the work of James Coleman and Maïder Fortuné, we find places of theatrical and cinematic reflexivity, but instead of interrogating the textual and cinematic material, as many artists do, they are interested in the movements of their central figures: the characters and the bodies of the actors. Their works are forged in the crucible of the performing arts. They appropriate the problems of the stage and replay them in the space of the image, which is conceived in genuinely theatrical terms.

Michael Snow

The deconstruction of the character and narrative is also central to the work of Michael Snow (Canada, 1929). A major figure in the history of experimental cinema, his videos constantly return to the motif of staged representation, and play with the codes, figures and loci of theatre. Several of his works question, for example, the roles attributed to the set in the creation of fiction, disrupting the references and the rules that underpin its organization. Thus, in *Preludes* (2000), a lateral travelling shot takes us into an interior that we surmise is a television studio. A group of young friends are spending the night together around a table, talking about violence and sex in the cinema, about fast food, and reacting to the debate with extreme and unexpected actions—a woman strips in front of the others, while the film closes with one of them throwing a jar that was part of the set down on the floor.

The confusion that arises when we try to follow the narrative is due to its speed (the whole thing lasts barely more than two minutes) and the discrepancy between image and sound

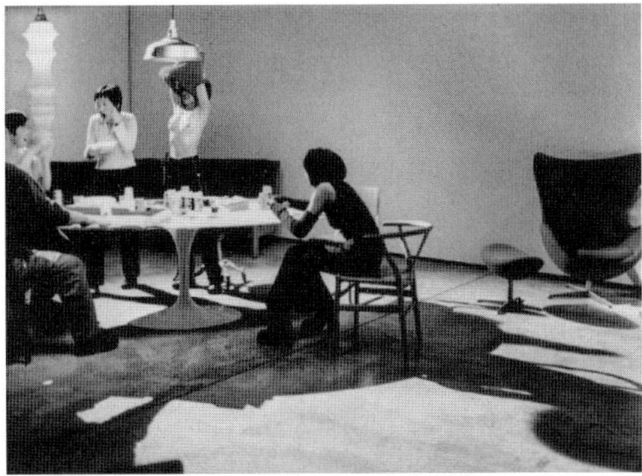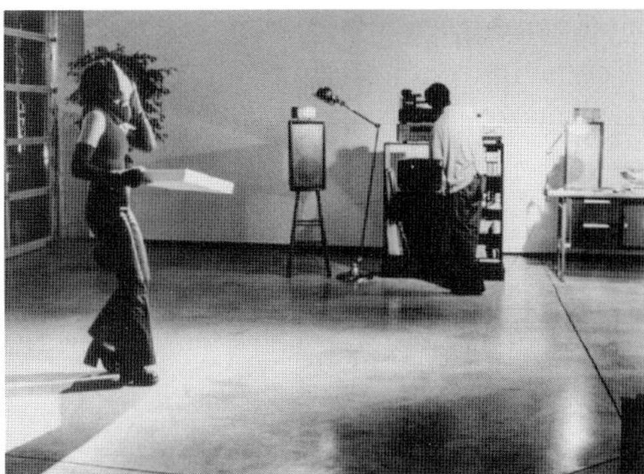

Michael Snow, *Preludes*, 2000. Colour, sound, 3'15. Courtesy of the artist.

that is created by the editing. The soundtrack starts with the sound of the jar smashing, which at this point is completely mysterious, and only becomes intelligible when the loop repeats and it recurs after the end of the film. Jacinto Lageira has analysed this effect of a visual and aural palindrome in terms of the 'Velázquez syndrome', combining the evocations of what has not yet happened, or is no longer happening, with the mirror in *Las Meniñas*, which introduces a temporal *mise-en-abyme*.[8] The viewer is thus confronted with a work whose setting (a very banal interior) and characters (young people, played by actors) are very banal, but whose rigid form is overturned by the editing. The 'Cut! Action!' we hear at the end of the film indicates the vocabulary of the film shoot, the better to undermine the power of words to make us believe in the image. The actors always seem as remote as ever from their character, and the more the video is repeated, the more the story recedes into the background.

Michael Snow plays frequently with the format of his films. He maintains the traditional boundaries constituted by the title and the credit sequence, the better to visualize the

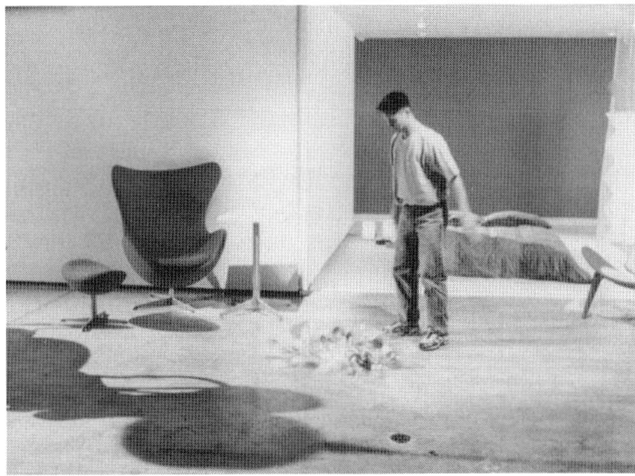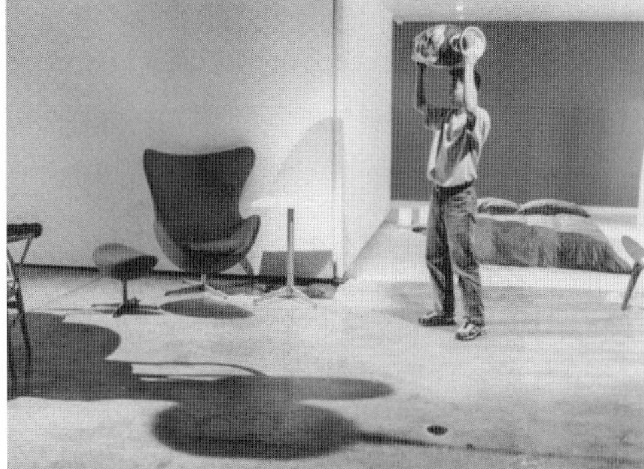

Michael Snow, *Preludes*, 2000. Colour, sound, 3'15. Courtesy of the artist.

temporal engagement needed to apprehend the work. At the beginning, viewers recognize the situations, the types of social relations, but are soon surprised by the excessiveness of the behaviour and disoriented by the general confusion that prevents them from grasping what is really happening and being said. It takes time to recapture the dramatic logic. The film is shown in a loop, not to make its beginning and end imperceptible, as is often the case in video works, but to mark the necessary repetition. The viewer is always well aware of the moment when the film starts and when it ends but even if they have seen the whole film, they also have the feeling that they have missed something: to have barely had the time to see the work. The speed of the exchanges and the brevity of the video, combined with the confusion of the reversed editing, means its reception is more complex. The beginning and end are signified only to mark their ineffectiveness because they are not the true markers of the duration of *Preludes*. The codes of the scenario are ironically maintained to mark the transition into another type of narrative that operates on the margins of the fictional language of cinema or television.

This is also the approach taken in *Sshtoorrty* (2005), a short video (less than two minutes) in front of which Michael Snow encourages us to be comfortably seated on inviting sofas.[9] The scenario is a banal story of jealousy between a woman, her lover and her husband, performed by Iranian actors in Farsi. The bourgeois interior is smooth and without relief; it does not retain the gaze. It provides no indications and does not help us to find our footing in a video shot in a language that we do not understand. This situation is of interest to Snow because it enables him to play with dialogue as abstract aural material, to exploit the resonant musicality of a language. Nevertheless, the meaning of the action quickly becomes clear because the situation is so caricatural that it is not necessary to understand the words being exchanged to grasp the content. The lover, an artist, comes to the couple's house to deliver a canvas they bought from him, and exchanges a surreptitious kiss with the woman in the hall. From the start, the painting focuses on the tension between the different characters, and when the lover offers to show the painting, to remove the packaging hiding it, it comes as no surprise that this scene ends with the husband revealing that he knows about his wife's infidelity. The handling of the canvas, which enters and exits the image several times, and the play of gazes over it, is extremely significant. The lover is like a bullfighter, provoking the husband with the painting and finally destroying it when using it to hit him with.

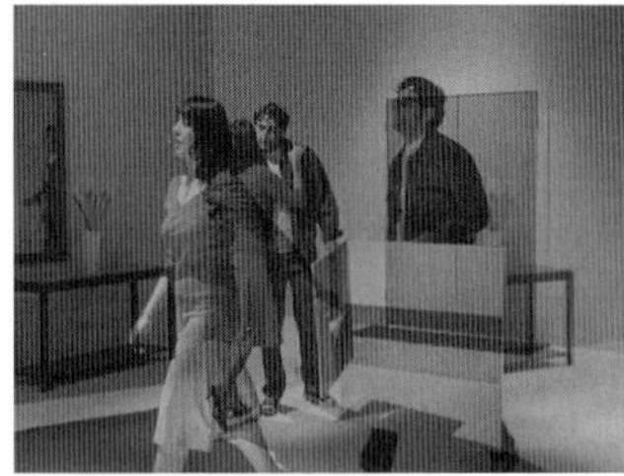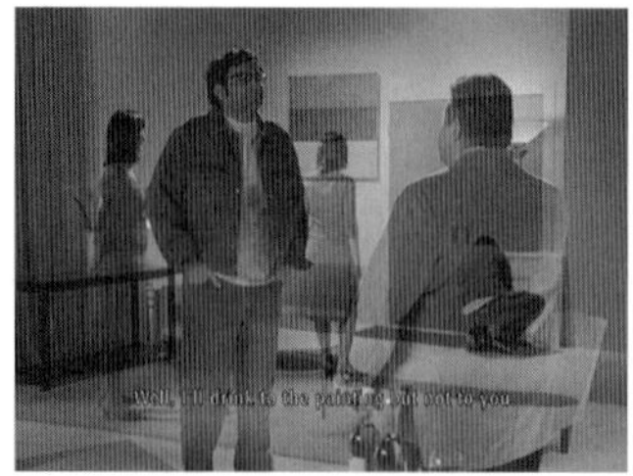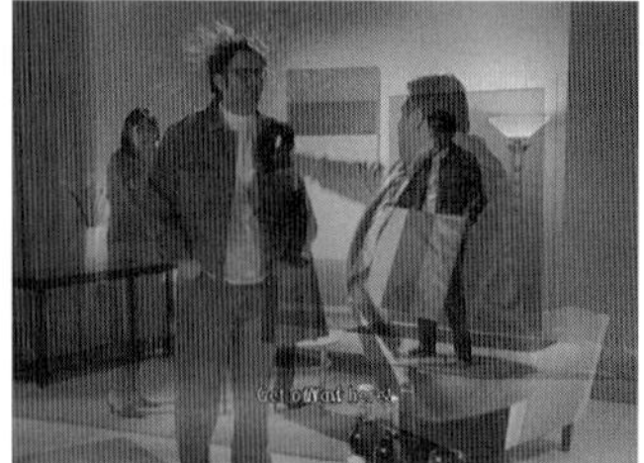

Michael Snow, *Sshtoorty*, 2005. Colour, sound, 20'. Courtesy of the artist.

The action in itself is of little interest, and attention soon starts to focus on the visual effects created by the editing. Snow effectively superimposed two halves of the film, using transparency, leaving only the first and last scenes isolated. Thus, there are always two moments of the story occurring at the same time, sharing the same spatio-temporality, which not only creates a visual confusion, but also creates plastic effects. The scene of the secret kiss by the door is thus juxtaposed with the image of the husband drinking a whisky, while he seems not to be seeing anything because he does not want to. This kind of confrontation manifestly echoes a possibly psychoanalytical reading of the situation, which we soon discard in favour of aesthetic appreciation. Beyond the rather slapstick effect, the construction of *Sshtoorrty* is also a piece of pictorial work on colours and forms. The contours are constantly flaring, disintegrating and redefining themselves in a fascinating visual movement. Snow also works with the medium of painting, and here he has fun changing the positions of the canvas and the video image because, as he puts it, painting becomes a 'moving picture because it moves all over the place', while the 'moving image' itself, video, is the place of pictorial work.[10]

Snow thus appropriates the television or film studio as a place for his meditation on the plasticity of the image, on the structures of narrative, and on the representation of human relationships. His works are striking in their ability to combine analytical reflection and aesthetic pleasure, to make these experiments with the gaze moments for the critical reading of narrative codes. The human figure remains central in the construction of the film but it is a figure voided of its substance, of its identity, leaving a mere caricature of a given type. It moves around in a unity of place that heightens the similarities with the theatre stage. Sitting on a sofa, spectators are positioned in a frontal relation to the images projected on a screen, a distanced relation that they are unable to escape. Snow has experimented with a variety of ways of shooting that will fragment vision, as in *The Central Region* (1971), in which a camera set to make unconventional movements was used to film on a deserted mountaintop in North Quebec. In an interview about the work given at the time, Snow noted, '[M]ost of my films accept the traditional theatre situation. Audience here, screen there. It makes

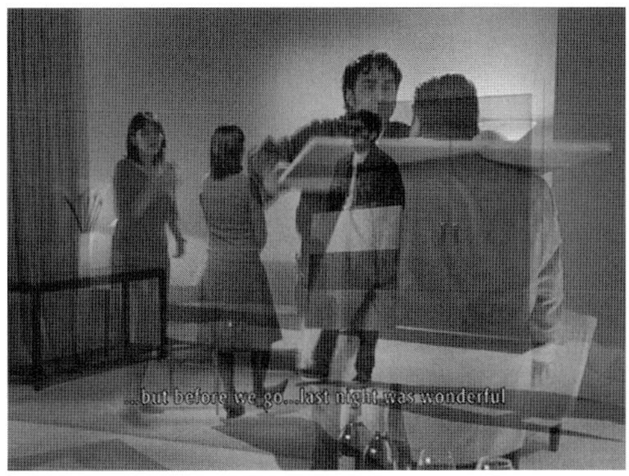

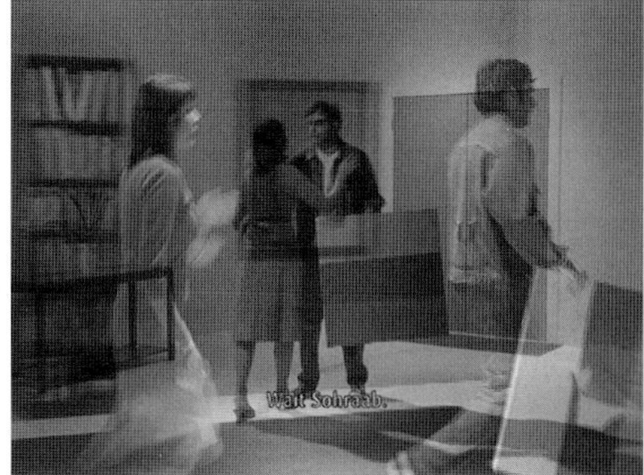

Michael Snow, *Sshtoortry*, 2005. Colour, sound, 20'. Courtesy of the artist.

concentration and contemplation possible. [...] Multiscreen things usually involve such vague optical direction that they're often a kind of therapeutical Impressionism'.[11] While I have no wish to become entangled in the kind of 'archaeology/critique' that tries to 'resuscitate living quotations' (which the artist personally warned me against), it is nevertheless interesting to consider the way in which Snow's work is grounded in a reflexive play on our relation to images. He is particularly attentive to its frameworks, its supports and if he now frequently works outside the traditional screen, he maintains a strong, questioning awareness of the places from which the image emerges.

Snow's initial rejection of the multisensorial model stemmed from his interest in what happens within the frame of the image, in its codes and structures and in its proximity to the language of the stage. Rather than seek to get the audience onto the stage, he questions its relation to the optical and symbolic mechanisms of vision. His many recent installations take a highly inventive approach to the screen surface. His very varied set-ups range from the use of a table or carpet as projection supports to the creation of translucent or deep screens, but they always maintain the image within a frame, however surprising its nature. His critique of multisensorial apparatuses anticipates the fascination with immersive images later evinced by numerous artists, multiplying screens, filling the exhibition space and giving the viewer no choice but to be drawn in by the seduction of visual and aural fluxes. And yet, it is not easy to occupy a space. It is not enough simply to fill it with images. In *Sshtoorrty*, the actors play in what is a completely staged environment, one very close to theatre. Here, video is a way of concentrating the gaze on what is at play in the representations, in the schemas of vision. Everything is fabricated, reminding us of the fictional constructions that structure the imaginary. This concern informing Snow's works is echoed by many artists who deploy the idea of the set in a practice of installation in which video is integrated into stage-like spaces that do not seek to captivate the viewer by immersing them in the image but, on the contrary, maintain them a state of awareness of their receptive position. Entering exhibitions by Jordi Colomer or Mika Rottenberg, we are invited into stage sets that affirm their status as such, indicating new modes of relation to the work.

'Inhabiting the Stage': Jordi Colomer and Mika Rottenberg

Approaching video while addressing the question of the scenographic space, artists like Jordi Colomer and Mika Rottenberg lead the viewer into a process of crossing the stage. By combining a projection device and sculptural installation with video images, they redefine the notion of the set. The experiences offered by the exhibition lead viewers to question their relation to the places of the image. The work of Catherine Sullivan (United States, 1968), especially *The Chittendens* (2005), typifies this exploration of the theatricality of the space of video by appropriating the stage and shifting it towards the exhibition. Laure Fernandez emphasizes this in her analysis, where she discusses the importance in the work of many artists of 'a questioning that is sometimes aesthetic, and often structural, of what the stage is, not as the space for a shared experience, but as a space distinct from that of the viewer'.[12, 13] The installation displaces into the exhibition the problems of the stage space, of the way it manages bodies and speech, of what is shown and what is concealed. Beyond this scenographic dimension, she puts in place another kind of relation to the space and reception of the work. When they enter an exhibition by Jordi Colomer or Mika Rottenberg, viewers move across a surface filled by an arrangement of different stages that are all places of representation. They can decide the rhythm of their movement in these spaces that are somewhere between backstage and stage. Continuing on from the subversion of the stage/auditorium (actor/spectator) distinction begun in the 1960s, these places avoid the spatial hierarchy of the raised stage and require a mobile spectator whose position is closer to that of the visual arts than to what is found in the theatre. However, by also standing apart from the question for sensorial fusion found in immersive art, the works under discussion here maintain the triangular author/work/spectator architecture of reception as defined by Hans Robert Jauss in his work on reception theory, giving visitors the chance to explore the in-between space of separation.[14]

Jordi Colomer

The videos of Jordi Colomer (Spain, 1962) are informed by reflections on architecture, the staging of the real and the construction of our lives' surroundings. The presence of the individual is central to his images and the landscapes take their meaning from the relation to the body located there. The aesthetic used is often close to that of documentary and the actors perform in his films more than they act. Familiar with the world of theatre, where he worked for a number of years, Colomer appropriates its places and codes. More generally, he develops in his works a reflection on the way in which we inhabit our private and collective life spaces, introducing an absurd dimension that echoes that of the real. His videos are inseparable from the installation set-ups that play a full role in shaping the viewer's experience. The exhibition space is reconstructed, fragmented by the play of openings and closures that oblige viewers to be conscious of their movements as they enter and exit the work. Imposing wooden structures frame the projections; unmatching coloured chairs both signal and enable the place of reception. Viewers are invited to move around the sets and thus to displace their relation to the work. Although attractive in a number of ways, the image intervenes only after this first experience of these structures that are a cross between sculpture and architecture, anchoring the gaze in a place. Colomer says that he is obsessed with the question of whether an actor on the stage or a spectator in an exhibition can inhabit a set.[15] His installations therefore always invoke the nature of the theatrical place as it is seen from backstage, the other side of the illusion. The fiction constructed by the video image combines with elements reminding us that it is a fabrication. Colomer thus tries to avoid a cinematic kind of fusion in which the room is darkened and the bodies of the viewers disappear when the screening starts.

In several of his pieces, he intervenes in public space, introducing surprising objects, such as a small-scale cast of the 'Popemobile' (*Papamóvil*, 2005–8), not with the aim of causing a stir (indeed, passers-by do no more than exchange intrigued looks) but more to question the capacity of everyday life to integrate something of the extraordinary and the imaginary. By his urban actions, Colomer expresses the fictional dimension of the real; beyond the comedy of the situation, his images make sense as interpretations of the world. When he questions us about our surroundings with his left-field poetic actions, like those of 'Father Coco' picking up various objects that he finds on his path, he breaks the fascination by introducing doubts about the sincerity and authenticity of the action.[16] Did Father Coco really find all the things in his bag when out walking? Where did the artist intervene? In his *Anarchitekton* series (2004), a man walks through various towns brandishing a cardboard model of the buildings around him, creating an effect of displacement and redundancy. The play of scales confirms the theatrical perspective. It encourages the viewer to take a distanced perspective on the real and grasp its fictional dimension.

If the world is conceived as a stage set, this is not so much to expose its reality as cardboard as it is to interrogate the mutual permeability between the real and the stage, the theatricality of the banal. This questioning has its origins in the 1960s with the beginnings of performance, particularly in the happenings of Allan Kaprow, and in the radical creations of the *Living Theatre*, who were the heirs of the carnival tradition in which everyone is an actor but without a stage or a show. In 1959, the American sociologist Erving Goffman published *The Presentation of Self in Everyday Life*, in which he used the vocabulary of theatre to analyse the development of the construction of identities and their relation to social life, demonstrating the validity of the theatrical model for the sociology of everyday life. Colomer's work is built on this heritage, which is particularly rich today in a society permeated by forms of entertainment. His videos do not, strictly speaking, generate a spectacle, for that is not the side of representation that interests him. He stages the other side, what he calls the 'parterre'.

For example, *Les Jumelles* (The Twins, 2001) is a two-channel video projection that takes us into the space of a theatre, facing the auditorium and its orange-red chairs. The cameras placed on the stage scan the space with lateral tracking shots and follow the actions of the twins who, after one of them has picked up the clothes left in the auditorium, try them on and swap them in front of the mirror. While they do so, the audience enter the theatre and calmly take their seats in the general hubbub, indifferent to what is taking place on the stage. When they suddenly disappear, the seats are again covered with forgotten clothes that one of the twins again picks up, thus completing the loop of the action. In this very short video, Colomer puts in place a poetic reflection on theatrical codes. He expresses this as follows, 'The twins inhabit the space between the stage and the parterre. Their action is invisible for the audience who, without realising what is going on, wait for the beginning of the show, talking, embracing and taking off their coats. No show is put on. The camera offers us a privileged perspective. We are, ultimately, spies watching these two worlds that a clear-cut line has separated for centuries: the stage, the actor's territory, and the auditorium, the space for the public. The theatre seen from inside. The action is repeated ad infinitum'.[17]

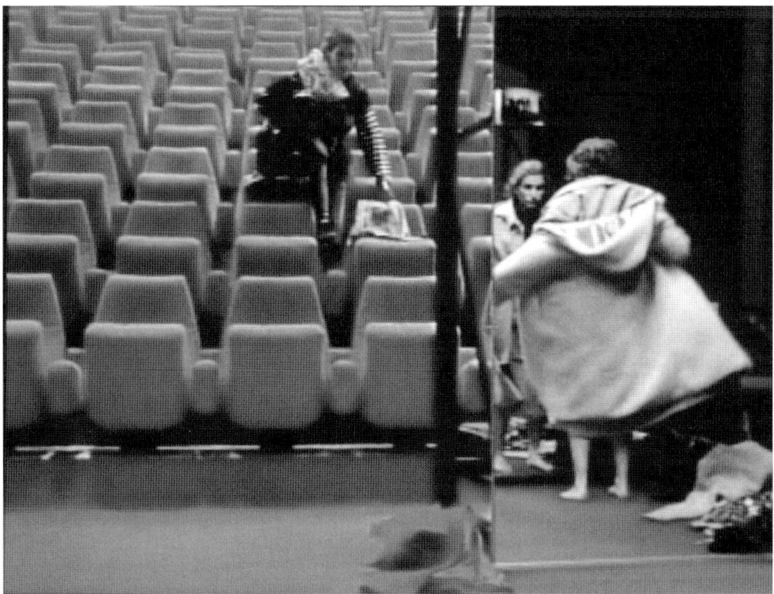

Jordi Colomer, *Les jumelles*, 2001. Video and projection room, 4'20, loop. Courtesy of the artist.

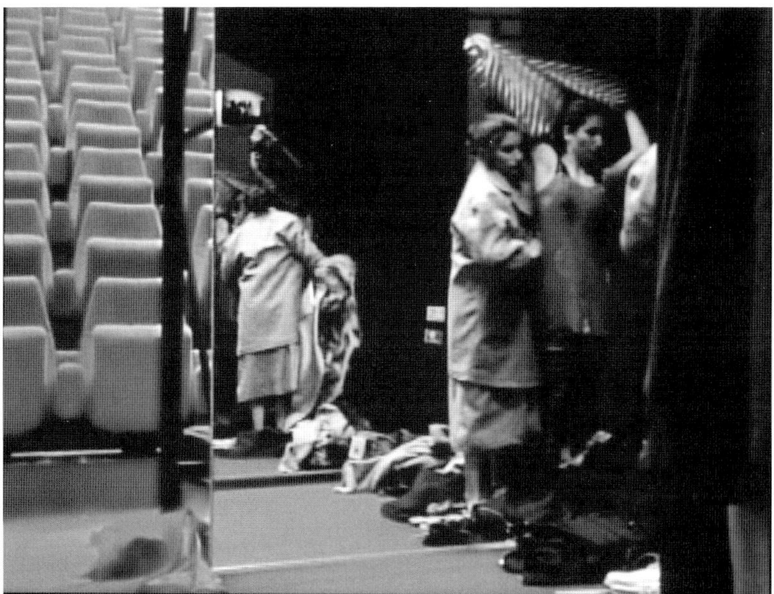

Jordi Colomer, *Les jumelles*, 2001. Video and projection room, 4'20, loop. Courtesy of the artist.

The frontier between these two worlds evoked by Colomer is clearly visible in the action, where the performance refuses to show itself on either side. The audience plays its own role while the twins stay hidden behind the mirror. The play of gazes is a perpetual delving into the self, and the viewers of this work, too, finds themselves facing their double through the presence of the audience. The stage/auditorium relation is reversed: the visible action is located not on the stage but in the lighted room, from which there comes a loud racket that is independent of the physical presence of the viewers. What we see, most of all, are the seats that accommodate the bodies, support the clothes and that people move between. The stage is not only obstructed by panels, but what happens there also seems strangely invisible. The audience does not see the twins. The last image before the film repeats shows the seats torn from their bases. *Les Jumelles* questions us about what happens in the theatre outside performances, and about the status of these moments. One thinks of *Office Edit II* (2001) by Bruce Nauman, in which the artist films his studio at night, when the mice come out. Their movements, crossing the images (it is a multichannel installation), their appearances and disappearances make the studio a new nocturnal stage. Colomer is interested in what goes beyond the traditional frame of theatre just as Nauman questions the space of the studio as a place for the creation of art. *Les Jumelles* is a poetic meditation on what goes on behind the scenes in a theatre, on the theatrical quality of the individual and collective actions, both banal and exceptional, that take place there, unwatched. The confrontation with theatrical architecture reflects, more than anywhere else, the theatrical character of everyday life.[18]

This idea is echoed in many of the projection structures that are part of the experience of Colomer's works. Whether a caravan, a sculpture or screen in breeze block or a cell, the viewer always has to enter a set. The reception device exteriorizes the relation to the film space, indicating the need to cross the threshold of the representation. Temporal experience is split between a sculptural aspect and an immersion in the video image. Numerous effects of *mise-en-abyme* link the two, as in *Simo* (1997), where the viewer enters a closed room that is the double of the one we see on the screen. We then go with a slow lateral travelling shot that follows the strange activity of Pilar Rebollar, a tiny actress, who is seen frantically opening a great number of shoe boxes, then filling them with jars of jam and, finally, going to sleep on a big carpet. Where viewers are isolated in the darkness of the screening cube, the actress busily enters and exits the room, paying no heed to the many people she passes on the way. Like her, all of them are crossing a space that we soon identify as a stage: one of them is on a ladder, probably to fix the lighting, while others are carrying props and costumes. The sound, a muffled buzz, heightens our impression that the actress is not in the same time frame as the other characters; that their respective spheres do not communicate. Viewers are in a similar state of reception, isolated in their gaze. Like her, they create their own bubble, far from the agitation of the visitors to the exhibition. They have the feeling that they are entering the set. Colomer often creates these fictional spaces that perturb the viewer's relation to the representation. Here, they are absorbed by the strange activity of a person with a singular physique who literally inhabits the set: her sleeping is very much the sign of her intimacy with the physical and mental cell that she inhabits. However, the

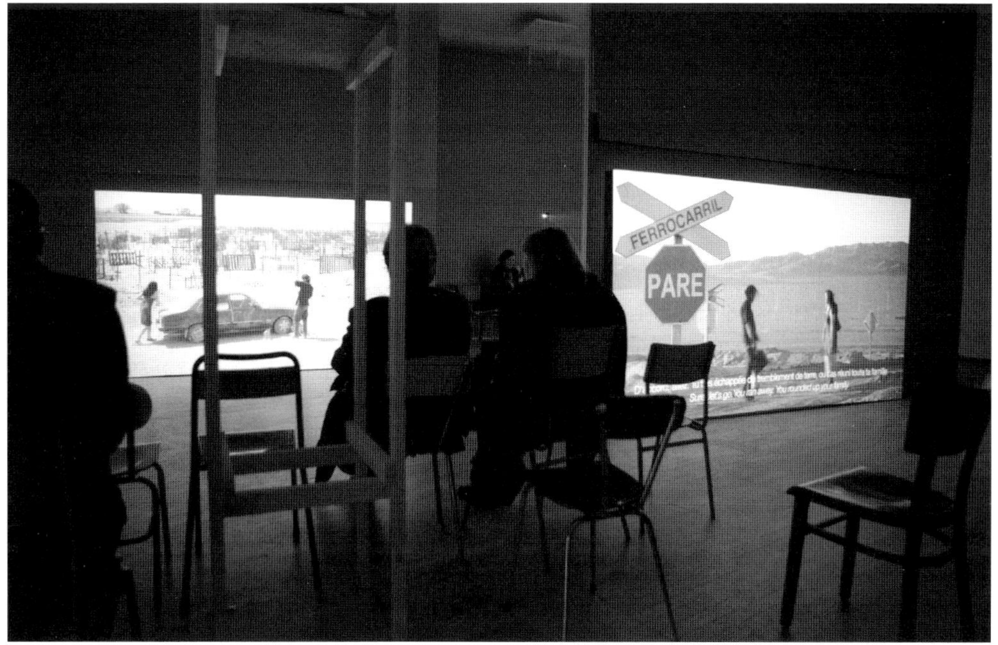

Jordi Colomer, *En la Pampa*, 2008. Installation view, Jeu de Paume, 2008, Paris. Five videos and projection room. Courtesy of the artist.

travelling shot reveals that there is no fourth wall in this room, and it seems less likely that the actress would really be able to feel isolated in an open space. The travelling shot, which already references the codes of construction of the cinematic image, reveals the trick photography and once more the fictional dimension of what we are being shown. Everything is constructed, acted, repeated, even if the scene has been displaced to the wings. The viewer is unsettled the moment another body enters *Simo*'s projection space, for this reminds them of their own isolation and prompts them to return to their own mobility.

In contrast to theatre or cinema, viewers are free to decide how long they spend in front of the projections, and to move round between the works. In Colomer's exhibitions, they also have the feeling that they are going behind the scenes of art-making, being invited to wander round the stages where fiction is made. *En la pampa* (2007) is emblematic in this respect, in that we see this video, shot with amateur actors in Chile's Atacama Desert, from crude tiered seats built with breeze blocks facing the four screens. While the man and woman in the film literally experience the idea of the world as a theatre, the installation set-up foregrounds the distancing effected by the video. The imposing structure counters the effect of closeness between the characters and the viewers, emphasizing the fact that, however minimally, the video is a construction. Still, for all their desire to create an image, the characters struggle to bring out the spectacular. The real temporality is too slow and only a few moments, such as the farewell scene, manage to create a degree of dramatic intensity. Generally, though, the

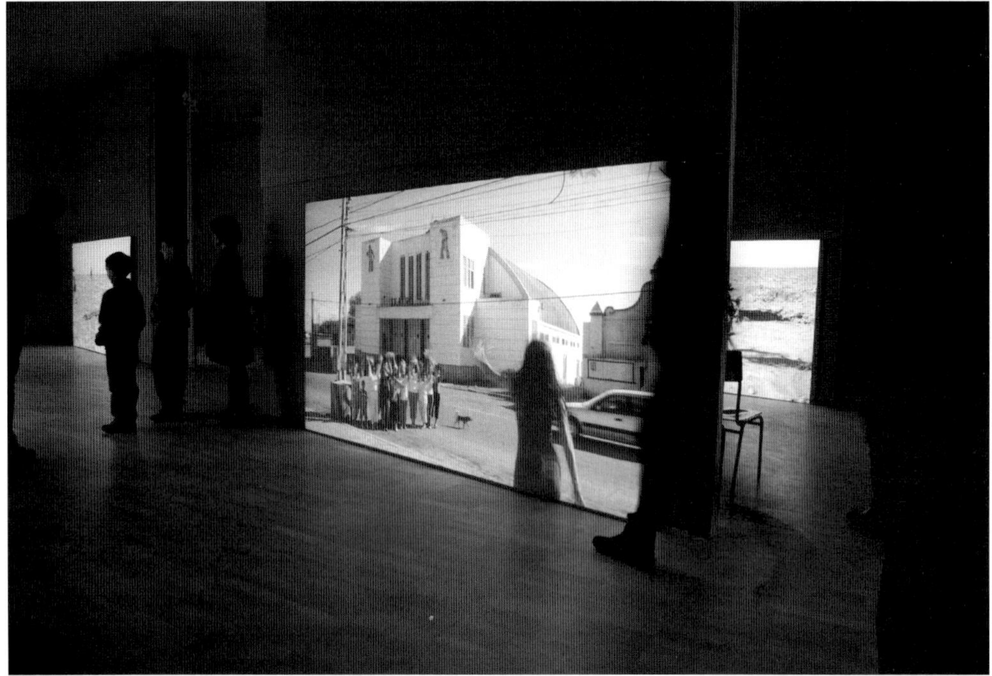

Jordi Colomer, *En la Pampa*, 2008. Installation view, Jeu de Paume, 2008, Paris. Five videos and projection room. Courtesy of the artist.

piece seems to bear out the words by Guy Debord that the actors are trying to memorize, 'Wandering in open country is naturally depressing'. With this piece, Colomer moves away geographically and tries to conceptualize the elsewhere of theatre by immersing himself in a space considered poor in narrative possibilities. He takes his camera and places the visitor in a cinematic-type relation, but this time, the real resists scenarization, despite the strangeness of the situations in which he places the actors, such as washing a car in the middle of the desert, carrying around a plastic Christmas tree.

Leaving the theatre to engage with outdoor urban space is a recurrent action in the work of Jordi Colomer. Every time he brings rules, scores, objects or maquettes that enable him to stage the real, 'I wanted to open the door of the stage—it was getting stifling in there— and get out into the street. One could say that afterwards, during their perambulations, my characters transported a fragment of the stage to see how it would transform perception of the city [...] or the desert'.[19] In *En la pampa*, boredom and emptiness dominate, and the repetition of the Debord quote fails to overcome a situation in which it is the case that chance is not met on the roadside. Inhabiting the stage becomes an existential question here, the question of inhabiting the world.

In this piece, Colomer deliberately takes a starting point that is as poor as possible, testing the capacity of the camera, of filmic construction, to shape the world. Viewers are confronted with their own desire for fiction, which gives form to the experience of things. The two characters act out in front of him the permanent quest for an event, for an encounter, for the irruption of something that gives life meaning by building the necessary setting. Immersed in these images via a scenographic apparatus that anchors them in the consciousness of their presence within a constructed space, viewers are also caught up in a questioning of the world as theatre.

Mika Rottenberg

The work of Mika Rottenberg (Argentina, 1976) has several points in common with Colomer's. It questions and extends the questioning of the registers of fiction present in the real. Based in the United States, Rottenberg devises extensive video installations, staging

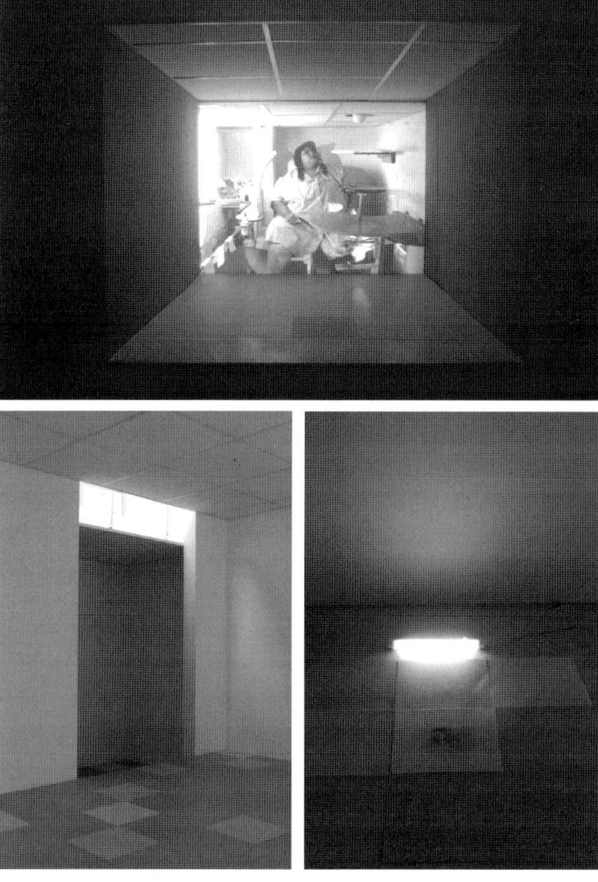

Mika Rottenberg, *(Big) Dough,* 2005–2009. Maison Rouge, Paris, 2009.
Courtesy the artist and Rosen Gallery, New York.

extreme manifestations of the real and constructing phantasmagorical visions. Characters with unusual physiques appear in visual universes conceived especially for them and take part in strange cycles of production arising from the specificities of the body.

This dynamic of energies is at the heart of Rottenberg's work: the formation of life, the process of perpetual creation, is observed in relation to its limit forms, its excesses. Rottenberg seeks out bodies that exist outside social criteria. Whether these phenomena are mastered or not, what they have in common is that they are all not only accepted, but also valorized for their work potential. The women Rottenberg works with make use of their abnormality by offering their services for films and photographs. They sell their difference using commercial strategies, but the thing about their monstrous-ness is that it is always linked to excessive development, to an unbridled corporeal production, due to nature or individual will: the women filmed have extraordinarily long hair or nails, are gigantic in size or have developed an exceptional musculature.

Rottenberg does more than just film the people she meets. These women live in environments conceived for their specificities, and the artist takes up this idea of constructing fictional spaces for them that are linked to their eccentricities, which distort the real by the play of echoes and ruptures. In *(Big) Dough* (2005–9), for example, women work on a production line, isolated in tiny rooms, with only holes allowing them to communicate. A very interesting, recurrent aspect of this organization is its verticality: the spaces staged by Rottenberg, in which these women work, reverse the usual logics of the horizontal chain of production. This modification enables her to withhold from our gaze a complete vision of the process, to isolate the phases, to accentuate isolation and to make transmission an act in which what is produced is often thrown away. In *(Big) Dough*, women transform an almost natural raw material—red varnished nails—into a shapeless paste packed in small quantities. Each stage is perfectly orchestrated in a knocked-up world that is ingenious but profoundly absurd. The paste spreads through a long tube from one floor to another, a viscously and powerfully kneaded form, while one of the women goes about breathing on a bed of artificial flowers, leading to the natural reaction of her sweating profusely and thus perfuming the paste. Each task creates a specific set of noises, a mixture of the mechanical and the human, and shows a combination of natural and artificial energies. As in Rottenberg's work, generally, everything takes place almost wordlessly, the exception being a few coded expressions linked to the organization of the work, as when one of them exclaims, 'I see it' on seeing the paste come down from her ceiling. This aside, there is no chat. Each person is isolated, and their communication boils down to their participation in a collective performance.

Rottenberg's world is highly feminine in terms of both of the characters she shows and the phenomena she takes as her starting points. Long nails and hair, attributes of femininity, are recurrent features. The artist expresses their fascination and the projections they allow. The works are strange, dreamlike drifts in which a caustic vision of capitalist societies combines with curiosity about the most surprising strategies of individual resistance. Rottenberg explains that it was seeing a cashier isolated behind her exotically decorated nails that led to the construction of a story in which the nails become the raw material of a completely crazy mode of economic organization.[20]

The relation to space is essential: a labyrinthine enclosure in *Cheese* (2007), a factory truck in *Tropical Breeze* (2004), a module of rooms in *(Big) Dough*. Every time, the body is in a sense enclosed, its secretions are sought and exploited. Viewers can enter into sculptures that echo the spaces in the film. In *(Big) Dough*, the ceilings are lowered, in some areas collapsed, and the ensemble gives an impression of a shaky structure. The gaze perceives the work within an illusionistic set-up that projects it into the filmic space, an effected heightened by the dimensions of the image, in which the characters appear actual size. The continuity between the ceiling in the video and the one in the projection space is disconcerting: a drop of water falls from the ceiling, as if the fiction were seeping from the set and infiltrating the reality of reception.

Everything is strange in Rottenberg's universe: the bodies, the actions, the living and working spaces, and yet a paradoxical impression of proximity and banality comes over us. The corporeal monstrosity of the actresses and the absurdity of the narratives fade and an atmosphere develops in which grating humour points up the excesses of contemporary societies while offering a very gentle vision of the humanity of these spectacular bodies. These women are victims of the collective crushing of the individual, where resistance means seeking out the exceptional along unexpected and terrifying paths. For the duration of the shoot, Rottenberg offers them a fellow feeling that enables them to construct tiny collective utopias. For example, in *Cheese*, the artist presents women with extremely long hair, living in a kind of enclosure in a generous and benevolent natural setting. This work was inspired by the magical tales of the seven Sutherland sisters, each of whom had an exceptional head of hair, as well as grace and musical qualities that made them famous. They were united and, together, had the business sense to exploit their renown, helping to create a real legend around their lives, which culminated in them building a big manor where they all lived together. *Cheese* uses numerous elements from this story, recreating an environment that evokes the nineteenth century (clothes, utensils, etc.). The magic of their gifts is emphasized here: raising goats and collecting water from the Niagara Falls, they make milk gush from the earth and sneeze real rabbits. Viewers experience this fable surrounded by a large wooden installation directly echoing the enclosure in the film.

In Rottenberg's work and in that of Jordi Colomer, viewers are anchored in the exhibition space in a permanent back and forth between immersion in the fiction and a return to the experience of reception. The installation of the video is part of a sculptural proposition that invites us to look at both the image and its setting. The travelling shots used by Colomer in *Les Jumelles* and *Simo* set up a dialogue between stage and room, theatre and studio. The mobility of the camera makes it possible to put the fictions on- and off-camera on the same level, and to constantly affirm the grounding of illusion in the set, in a fabrication. The camera is not subjective. It is within the codes of cinema, within the code of the travelling shot, that this deconstruction takes place. Viewers are invited to operate in the same way in their own experience of vision, to alternate viewpoints. The installation is a kind of extension, an excrescence of the fictional in the exhibition space through the presentation of props and elements from the set. This set-up recalls the way performances are presented in museums, where artists exhibit 'dead things' from their actions, questioning their ability to tell us about what happened.[21] However, here there is more than just the authenticity of the set: the confinement of *(Big) Dough* is not exactly the same as the one in the film, and there is no attempt to make us believe it is. Unlike the performance, the point is not to evoke a past moment by staging objects telling us that 'this has been', but to create a sense of involvement, a feeling of familiarity, between the place of the exhibition and that of the shoot. Rottenberg, too, makes abundant use of travelling shots, and the construction of *(Big) Dough* evokes another video by Colomer, *Le dortoir* (The Dormitory, 2002), in which the camera circulates between different parts of a factitious building the day after a party (people dozing, empty cans and garlands set the scene). As in *(Big) Dough,* the camera has the power to go through walls and ceilings, to circulate between different spaces, to offer us an omniscient vision. By extending the set into the exhibition space, Rottenberg invites the viewer onto the stage. The point is not to create a perceptual uncertainty, to play with illusion but, on the contrary, to affirm the scenic dimension of the filmic space and the exhibition venue. In a visual culture dominated by the spectacular image, the work of Colomer and Rottenberg constitutes a real commitment to reflection on the construction of the visible: far from eulogizing the fabrication of illusion, they very humorously expose its mechanisms.

Notes

1   Hans-Thies Lehmann, *Postdramatic Theatre*, Routledge, 2005, p. 26. Original German edition, *Postdramatisches Theater,*Verlag der Autoren, 1999.

2   Jean-Pierre Ryngaert and Julie Sermon (eds.), *Le personnage théâtral contemporain: décomposition, recomposition*, Théâtrales, 2006.

3   Jean-Louis Besson (ed.), *L'acteur entre personnage et performance. Présences de l'acteur dans la representation contemporaine*, Centre d'Études Théâtrales, 26/2003, Université Catholique de Louvain.

4   On this point, see Béatrice Picon-Vallin (ed.) *Les écrans sur la scène*, L' Age d'Homme, 2009.

5   Jean Fisher, 'The Place of the Spectator in the Work of James Coleman', in *James Coleman*, October Files, Baker, 2003, p. 32.

6   'Le "Film" de James Coleman', Raymond Bellour, in 'D'un autre cinéma', *Trafic n° 34*, été 2000, p. 5 à 21.

7   Hans-Thies Lehmann, *Postdramatic Theatre*, op. cit., p. 12.

8   Jacinto Lageira, 'Le syndrome de Velázquez', *Parachute 103*, 7-8-9- 2001, p. 72–85.

9   I am referring to the installation of the work in *Solo Snow*, the solo exhibition of Michael Snow at Le Fresnoy (Tourcoing, France) in 2011.

10 Interview given during the exhibition *Solo Snow* at Le Fresnoy, Tourcoing, 11 February 2011.

11 'Converging on *The Central Region*: Michael Snow in Conversation with Charlotte Townsend', *artscanada 28, 1, 152/153 (1971)*, reprinted in *Collected Writings 1958-2001. Michael Snow*, Wilfrid Laurier University Press, 2010, p. 54.

12 This work should have been discussed in this study. However, not having been able to experience it for myself, I prefer not to evoke it and let readers discover it for themselves.

13 Laure Fernandez, 'L'espace dramatisé de l'installation vidéo: *The Chittendens* de Catherine Sullivan, une autre scène pour le théâtre', in *Figures de l'art no. 18, L'œuvre en scène ou ce que l'art doit à la scénographie*, 2010, Presses Universitaires de Pau, p. 102.

14 Hans Robert Jauss, *Toward an Aesthetic of Reception*, University of Minnesota Press, 1982.

15 'Habiter le décor', Jordi Colomer, *Pavillon no 2*, Monaco, Ecole d'Art et de Scénographie, 2009, p. 62–71. The title of the chapter 2 of this book, 'Inhabiting the Stage', is a citation of Jordi Colomer's text.

16 *Father Coco and Some Lost Objects in 2001* (5', 2002).

17 *Father Coco and Some Lost Objects in 2001* (5', 2002).

18 This video also happened to be shot in the disused theatre at the Villa Arson art centre and school in Nice, where Jordi Colomer was in residence at the time. The theatre was closed shortly after its construction because of technical problems, and its ghostly presence behind the current lecture room makes it particularly well suited to projections and reflections on what goes on 'behind the scenes.'

19 Conversation between Marta Gili and Jordi Colomer, 'Habiter le décor', in *Fuegogratis*, exh. cat. by Jordi Colomer, Paris: Le Point du Jour/Jeu de Paume, Paris, 2008, p. 166.

20 I refer to the talk given by Mika Rottenberg at La Maison Rouge in Paris on 19 February 2009, during her solo show there.

21 On this point, see the exhibition catalogue *Ne pas jouer avec les choses mortes*, Nice/Dijon, Villa Arson Nice and Les Presses du Réel, 2009.

Chapter 3

Theatres of Projection

Exhibiting the Video Image

Exhibiting filmed images is now a central concern for museums and art centres, which need to fit their structures round the specificities of this medium. Hence, the creation of permanent screening rooms offering decent conditions for the reception of videos, thanks to equipment conceived on the model of cinemas. Whether showing programmes or a single work, these spaces reflect the shift in video towards HD format, with production conditions closer to those of cinema. As early as the 1980s, many artists began looking beyond the artisanal world of early video and to aim for more professional means of production. The quality of the images and sound improved and editing software became easier to use, giving them greater technical autonomy, and this general development made it logical for museums to create specific spaces going beyond simple monitor display. In the early 1990s, the falling cost of video projectors accelerated these changes, as museums found it easier to adopt the new technologies and thus offer modes of display closer to cinema. Specific video spaces became increasingly frequent, often on the edge of the exhibition rooms (in the museum entrance or in the basement). Viewers could watch in comfort, away from the flow of visitors. Such spaces meet the needs of works that are very close to the cinema in both their production and display, and whose duration, which is sometimes considerable, requires concentration and therefore conditions that are rarely compatible with the mobility of bodies and gazes in the usual exhibition space. The main drawback of such special set-ups is that video tends to become excluded from the collective exhibition. Many visitors do not take the time to end or begin their visit with the video displays, especially when their space is clearly separated from the gallery spaces, as is the case, for example, at the Jeu de Paume in Paris.[1] In contrast, the use of picture walls and screens within the main galleries helps properly include videos in the general exhibition sequence, so that they can dialogue with the other works. This kind of display is often used for silent films, as was the case in the Pompidou Centre exhibition *Le Mouvement des Images* in 2006–7. *Hand Catching Lead* by Richard Serra, a film of the artist's hand trying with mixed success to catch small sheets of lead, and light experiments by Lazlo Moholy-Nagy, projected on the picture walls were perfectly integrated into the general exhibition sequence. The repetitive nature of the actions involved and the short duration of the films and videos lent themselves to this immersion. But for many pieces, sound quality is too important for them to work in such a context.

Another solution—seen, again, in *Le Mouvement des Images*—is to install screening rooms within the exhibition space, a series of immersive black boxes punctuating the hanging, protected by opaque curtains. These mini-cinemas offer numerous opportunities to see films, experimental shorts, artists' videos and excerpts from features. The museographic interest is clear, and this system is generally quite effective. At the same time, what it does is simply transpose the conditions of traditional cinema into the museum. And, as we have seen, what the move away from cinema theatres involves is calling into question the fixed model of cinematic reception, and the rejection of a situation of submission described thus by Roland Barthes, that of the viewer 'burying himself in (…) a dim, anonymous, indifferent cube where that festival of affects known as a film will be presented'.[2] In bringing the moving image into the exhibition space, artists find new conditions of reception that offer a different kind of relation to the viewer, positioning them at the centre of the experience. The point is not to bring cinema into the museum, but to offer modalities of immersion in images. The spectator becomes, as Dominique Païni has analysed with reference to Baudelaire, a '*flâneur* of installations, in the same way as we say a forest walker or *promeneur* on the Grands Boulevards, attracted, and at the same time resisting, these images that escape any goal other than their own looping'.[3] As Païni insists in this essay, *Le temps exposé. De la salle au musée*, this state of unpressured strolling can often be a trap. The desire to capture the visitor's attention has all too often led video makers to overindulge the spectacular effects of slow motion, the aesthetic effects of high definition, and the sheer scale of the installation. The criticism here is not just artistic, but concerns the general relation to the effects of spatialized, multichannel images, and the need to create meaningful display devices. And indeed, many artists do manage to avoid a fetishistic approach to the moving image in their museum video installations, using spatialization to bring out the perceptual mechanism of the time image and, more broadly, to probe at the relation of mind and body to the moving image.

Thinking Space and Projecting the World

> The scenographer (…) seeks to break free of the conventional museum framework by frequently choosing non-museum venues, and takes an interest in the aesthetic relation as form, that is to say, in the organization of space between the works and the public. He considers the exhibition as a way of staging both the works and the viewers.
>
> Jérome Glicenstein, *L'art: une histoire d'expositions*, 2009, p. 16

The definition of scenography proposed by Jérome Glicenstein posits a theoretical framework that exceeds that of the simple management of a space and expresses its aesthetic, cognitive and political underpinnings, as observed when it is explored according to the logic of research. The scenographic projects for video that we are going to consider partake of these dynamic, inventing innovative presentation devices for the works by infusing them with artistic and theoretical concerns. In order to exhibit the moving image, the scenographer must find solutions that take into account the needs of visitor movement, the productive dialogue to be maintained between the works, and the need to nevertheless preserve each work's visual and aural autonomy. The difficulty is much greater when the exhibitions show exclusively this kind of work. Artists have addressed these questions, approaching exhibition design as a creative territory in its own right, their research going beyond the effective presentation of their own works. Extending the logics of the installation, these are projection spaces that raise the question of the spectator's body, of their habits with regard to moving images, and the quality of their presence in a space.

Expanded cinema is the historic term for films that reject the model of the traditional screen and experiment with other projection supports. Questioning conventional exhibition structures, these works continue the heritage of Dadaist actions and their break-out from museum structures, their challenging of the artistic object and aesthetic qualities and immersion in cabaret, the street and life generally. The beginnings of expanded cinema paralleled the first happenings and Fluxus events, asserting a strong relation to the body, the spectator, the present moment and the place of the action. As of the 1960s, projections began to be made outside cinemas and galleries, in a search for new spaces, new supports and, more fundamentally, other kinds of relations to the moving image. A collective book, *Expanded Cinema. Art, Performance, Film*, meets a very real need to rethink that crucial period, when the language of what we now call 'video installation' was put in place.[4] Art history records the *Exploding Plastic Inevitable*, put on in 1966 by Andy Warhol with the Velvet Underground in New York, combining music, performance, film projections and other artistic materials, generating a new form and exploring the capacity of the visual work to inhabit the stage. *Expanded Cinema. Art, Performance, Film* also does justice to the experiences offered by other artists in the United States and in the United Kingdom, such as Stan Vanderbeek, Carolee Schneemann, Malcom Le Grice and Annabel Nicolson. All these artists are well known as key figures in the history of experimental cinema and activist performance, but less so for their interest in the space of projection. And yet, as Carolee Schneemann told Duncan White in an interview, from the mid-1960s onwards what she was trying to do in her performance projections was 'compact these small intense images and then reconstruct space with them. A space within, in which I can also activate movements, objects'.[5] By studying this history, one comes to realize that the space in, on and through which video images came to life was an important consideration right from the start. In rural New York, for example, Stan Vanderbeek bought a grain silo and fitted the top out with projectors to make it the support of multiple images. This was the famous Movie Drome, activated in 1966, where visitors were invited to come and lie on its floor to watch the projection, a gigantic moving collage of images and sounds combining found material and auteur films. This landmark event has gone down in the annals of experimental cinema, even if technical problems meant that the session had to be curtailed and was not repeated.[6] Another problem for Vanderbeek was the interference between the noise of the projectors and the sound of the films, as well as between the plastic material of the silo surface and the images. As this case shows, the desire to get away from the conventional framework of cinema, to find a place in the materiality of the world, in the continuous, multiple flux of sensations, stands in contradiction to the requirement for the work to be autonomous. How, after all, does one conceive such a projection space without then taking into account its constraints in the elaboration of the work itself? Vanderbeek seems to have underestimated the effects of his Movie Drome, which initiated a real risking of the video image outside its accredited spaces. This problem is still of concern today, and the reticence is just as great when it comes to inscribing a video work in public space; such are the risks of the soundtrack becoming distorted or the conditions of projection impaired that few artists are prepared to venture into spaces outside the gallery or museum, unless using giant screens. However, a number of spaces have been created to offer experimental conditions for the reception of video outside the museum, such as Vidéo K and the Hbox, which are discussed later.

In the 1960s, the explorations of expanded cinema went hand in hand with political engagement, a concern to find other forms of expression so that one could speak to the viewer outside the museum, or in radical forms that challenged their passive reception. This was the idea behind Schneemann's *Snows (Kinetic Theatre)* (1967), a collective performance in which images—taken from European press coverage of the Vietnam War—were projected on the actual bodies of the participants. In this way, two different realities interpenetrated in the collages made on the performers' bodies. The audience, who at first seemed comfortably settled outside the action, later found that their gestures of acceptance or protest had been recorded by sensors hidden under the seats, driving changes in the rhythm of the projections. The public's unconscious involvement was a way of challenging its indifference towards political realities that, even if not occurring in the same space, did occupy the same time. The set-up was designed to disrupt the foundations of the gaze and the commonplaces of representation. In a text written at this time, 'Culture: Intercom', Stan Vanderbeek describes a dream of his that he wanted to come true: the creation, thanks to expanded cinema, of a new language that would serve to bring art closer to life, and thus open the way to a new society, a future called 'Ethos-Cinema'.[7] If this vocabulary now seems dated, this militant, even utopian dimension of expanded cinema is worth bearing in mind. By experimenting with the projection space, artists questioned the codes and formats that condition our relation to the world, initiating a political reflection on images.

The Scenography of Video Exhibitions

When artists started using video, television represented an influential model, and their productions were conceived as a usually critical appropriation of its codes. And because the monitor long remained the most common means of showing these works, the viewer's relation to the images seemed at first glance to be the same as for television. This sensation of closeness decreased as the use of video projectors became more widespread in museums, but has now returned because of the democratization of this technology and its presence in many homes. The resemblance between artist's videos and the moving images found everywhere in our way of life has thus brought into being a creative field that plays on the confusion between the two. Artists have conceived installations for showing their videos that create a relation between the exhibition space and domestic space, an emblematic example being *Das Zimmer* (1994) by Pipilotti Rist. Visitors are invited to enter a gigantic salon, to sit down on a huge sofa and use a massive remote control to surf through the artist's videos. In this way, Rist appropriates the private sphere, everyday actions, and transposes them into the exhibition space. Viewers are welcomed into a place reminiscent of their own familiar world, but one that will be overturned by the contents of the works they view. By surfing the videos, they may have the impression that they are reasserting the ability to choose what they see, although in reality they are simply confined in a false freedom, unable to escape a closed programme, just as they are with their television.

In this piece, Rist is questioning cultural habits in our relations to moving images. The sofa, coffee table, lamp and TV set an everyday scene and reflect back the habits of looking that are rooted there. By bringing them into the exhibition space, Rist plays with the apparent closeness of artist's videos to TV productions, while showing, through our sensation of being physically crushed by the oversized objects, the passive, consumerist position of the TV viewer. How, then, do we find modalities for exhibiting the video image that avoid this trap, that take viewers away from the habits of their gaze? The subversion of models of dissemination is a recurrent way of interrogating perceptual patterns, testing the capacity of the video image to take over the exhibition space by setting the gaze in motion.

Fabrice Gygi's *Vidéothèque Mobile*

In 1998, the Centre Culturel Suisse in Paris put on a show of contemporary Swiss video art, *Dogdays Are Over*, curated by Nicolas Trembley. One featured artist, Fabrice Gygi (born 1965), has links to the alternative milieu whose radical, provocative work affects fecund displacements between popular festivity and gatherings and the art scene. He appropriates structures used for collective events—tiered seating, tents, rostra—and integrates them into a project that critiques the tools for organizing communal space. The materials he uses convey a cold, destabilizing atmosphere, taking us onto a terrain where the dominant ideologies are challenged through a focus on their auxiliary tools. His work is thus fairly distant from the aesthetic of Sylvie Fleury or Pipilotti Rist, who also featured in the show. His videos, raw documents made during his performances, would have sat strangely with the collective project. His contribution this time, then, did not consist of previous works but in the construction of a mobile videotheque. The idea was to offer a viewing space with access to a wide choice of videos, and to broaden the curatorial offering. Gigi's works often set up links with counter-culture, in a dialogue between different spheres of creation. If the videos shown in the *Vidéothèque Mobile* were works produced or assembled by Swiss public collections, and were not strictly speaking representative of alternative culture, the militant dimension of this project resided in Gigi's proposition to host other works within his own.

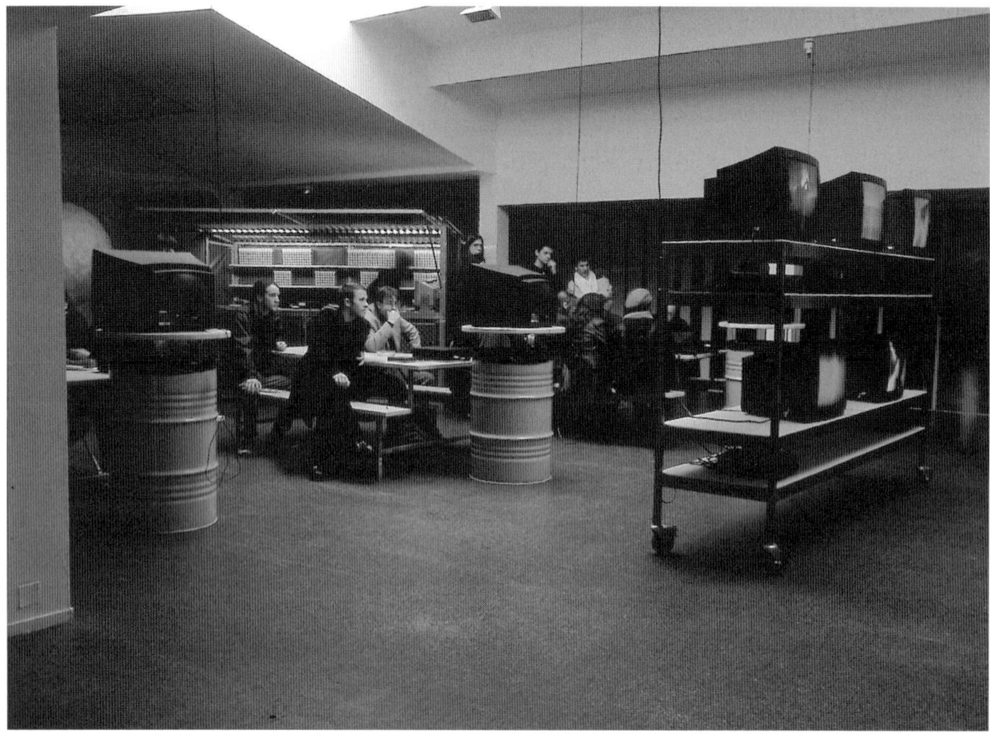

Fabrice Gygi, *Vidéothèque mobile*, 1998. Collection FRAC Ile-de-France. Courtesy of the artist and gallery Chantal Crousel.

That is what most deeply links this piece, which has remained isolated, with the rest of his work, as he readily admits.[8]

Materially, the *Vidéothèque Mobile* comprises a stand and wooden tables with matching benches and tiers. Visitors are encouraged to come up to the stand and order one of the videos, then to watch it at one of the tables or on the shelves. The ensemble is thus perfectly suited to the needs of a group show, enabling visitors to discover the riches of the programme at their own pace, freely choosing what they want to watch. They also benefit from the advice of the mediator behind the bar and, thanks to DVD (originally VCR), enjoy a very close relation to the videos, similar to domestic use. The large number of works and the absence of suggested viewing order can be interpreted as an appeal to visitors' responsibility with regard to choosing what they want to take the time to watch. However, the overall openness of the *Vidéothèque Mobile*, which is not divided up into individual spaces as one might have expected, means that one cannot recreate the isolation of a living room; instead, it creates zones of intrusion. A spectator viewing a work can be joined by others who come to sit at their table, attracted by the images or the sound. This situation recalls Gigi's interest in popular festivities and their spontaneity of interaction. For all that, the piece is not an example of the relational aesthetics that were in vogue at the time of its production, and that conceived the artistic experience as a space of discussion and encounter. Gygi used metal shelves, wooden tables and recuperated jerricans, not comfortable carpets and cushions. The conviviality associated with the big tables was quickly undermined by their use, showing this work's fertile contradictions.

The *Vidéothèque Mobile* now belongs to the FRAC Ile-de-France and is frequently presented in spaces not designed for exhibitions, such as the entrance to the Paris-Belleville architecture school in 2007. The surprising thing here was its apparent failure to generate much collective energy. However, in fact, it is no easier to enter into contact with one's neighbours in this setting than it is in the new media space at the Pompidou Centre in Paris, which was clearly designed for the individual viewing of artists' videos. The description of the piece says that the stand could be used to distribute drinks as well as videos, and that the jerrican tables could be used for both at the same time. However, this rarely happened, and visitors ended up alone at the wooden table, trying to amplify the sound to offset the difficulties of concentration linked to the space, occupied by other activities as well as the piece. With no headphones, and given the discomfort of the wooden benches, and the excessive distance from the monitors of the tiered seating, viewers struggled to find decent conditions for looking at the work. Gygi has never claimed to be an exhibition designer, and it may be inappropriate to consider his piece in those terms. Let us venture the hypothesis that, in the tension with its status at FRAC Ile-de-France, the *Vidéothèque Mobile* also offers a critique of the projection spaces set aside for video.

By a change of perspective, the idea of transportability stated in the title seems very ironic, because the structure is extremely heavy and bulky, when a monitor and headphones would suffice to play the videos. Here, the tables, jerricans, tiers and metal structures complicate access to the works and disrupt the mobility of a very light artistic form. Unnecessary, and antithetical to the minimalist space of the Centre Culturel Suisse for which they were conceived, the elements making up the *Vidéothèque Mobile* impose a sculptural approach. The support is not forgotten so as to facilitate immersion in the videos; on the contrary, it is constantly reminding us of its presence. It places us beside the works, displacing our relation to the image by keeping us from losing ourselves in the what we see. The gaze is constantly attracted by the sound of the other videos being viewed, disturbed by the noise of viewers sitting down or crossing the room without stopping. The work constructed by Gygi plays with the utopia that informed video art in the 1960s: the confidence in what was thought to be an improved mobility of this medium outside artistic fields. Many artists tried to explore this porosity between video and television by producing works that are broadcast on the small screen, thanks to collaboration with existing programmes, with teams that are open to experiment. In 1969, Gerry Schum, the producer of a television-based gallery in Germany, wrote excitedly about the way video was allowing art to escape, 'the eternal triangle of studio, gallery, collector, in which it has moved up to now. Instead of art as private property, which prevents the circulation of artworks, communication with a wider audience is now possible thanks to televised broadcasts or repeats'.[9] Gygi's *Vidéothèque Mobile* seems to share the same enthusiasm, offering the experience of works in a non-museum, but what it most shows is the failure of that dream.

The idea of a portable museum is not new. Marcel Duchamp and, after him, Robert Filliou, both moved away from the idea of the unique artwork. Video, an eminently reproducible medium, had the qualities required to take art outside its usual territories. In Duchamp's *La Boîte-en-valise* (1936–41) and Filliou's *La Galerie légitime* (1961), the works were all small or miniaturized so that they could be held in a case or hat and be transported. The irony and subversion of these undertakings were obvious, as they are in Rist's *Das Zimmer*, where the gigantic furniture and objects make the television and the images shown on it look tiny. The problem of scale also arises when one takes position on the tiers of the *Vidéothèque Mobile*, which are oversized in relation to the monitors. Video is not at the centre of the experience of the work, it is part of a whole that takes the viewer away from the relation of fascination to the movement of the images. In this piece, Gygi offers a reflection on conditions of reception and on the commonplaces that underpin it.

Because it asserts a powerful spatio-temporal dimension, and obliges the viewer to inhabit the place of the experience, video is in fact not a medium that circulates easily. Few of the many attempts to displace artworks outside the museum, to install them in public places, to show them on advertising screens or in vitrines, could be considered a great success. Only a small proportion of video works can venture outside the exhibition space. One factor that helps is proximity with popular culture, the ability to manipulate its codes. The great majority of these works fails to make this transition, for they require a state of mental and physical receptiveness that is hard to achieve outside the museum, in places where the gaze is distracted and fleeting. To exist in the city, works must develop a specific way of managing space, so that sight can be attracted and drawn in by a total experience. Doug Aitken's *Frontier* (2009) appears to meet this challenge perfectly.[10] Constituted by a white cube pierced with openings, the work stood on Tiberina Island in Rome. From the outside, it gave the impression of a vibrating, shifting volume, sending out light through its openings. Inside, multiple projections offered an alternation of wide and narrow views that took viewers on an imaginary journey, in the footsteps of a character played by Ed Ruscha. By virtue of its horizontal openings onto the city, the space installed the work in a dialogue with the exterior, offering passers-by on the bridge connecting the island to the riverbank the intriguing sight of a cube filled with images. Visitors were immersed in the videos, combining the journeys through the multiple landscapes in the films with the backdrop of the city. The fragmentation of vision was driven by this confrontation between fiction and the real, further disorienting the viewer by placing them before a complex, plural and tormented world, and engaging the body in an erratic progress. The work porously installed in public space affirms its own provenance, inciting the viewer through aesthetic emotion to undertake a reflection on the state of disorientation that constructs our perception of the world.[11] By cutting through the walls of the white cube, by immersing it in the city, Aitken affirmed the spatio-temporality of an experience that cannot be detached from the present and the place where it occurs.

Vidéo K: A Special Case

In the early 2000s, the Délégation aux Arts Plastiques (The visual arts wing of the French Ministry of Culture) and the Centre d'Art le Parvis in southwest France made an innovative and ambitious commission for a structure to house artists' videos outside conventional exhibition spaces. This was motivated by the realization that, despite its closeness to the television image, video was struggling to exist in public space. This structure would be a module that could be set up in temporary locations disconnected from artistic institutions, but not so much a mobile structure as a multiple one, a structure that could be duplicated and be durably installed in various public places. The first pilot project, Vidéo K, was conceived in relation to the specific situation of Le Parvis, an art centre with twin spaces in Pau and Tarbes, in the Pyrenees region, housed and financially supported by the Leclerc group. In Tarbes, it is located on the mezzanine of a shopping centre, where it remains relatively secluded amidst the commercial activity because of the difference of level. Even more radically, Vidéo K installed in the Leclerc hypermarket in Pau stood in the space between the checkouts and the car park, the idea being to take advantage of the high frequentation of the area and enable communication between the artistic and commercial spaces. Three teams submitted architectural projects, and the winner was the proposal by the French architect and designer Claire Petetin, which she defined as a 'house of images'.[12,13]

Vidéo K was above all a shelter, an opaque volume covered with a translucent skin in an attractive fluorescent pink colour. The idea was to create a simple form comprising two interlocking boxes, with a slight gap between them where the technical equipment could be fitted. From the outside, Vidéo K is intriguing and engaging by virtue of its luminous power that stands out from the ubiquitous commercial signage and asserts a marginal identity, successfully drawing the gaze and encouraging passers-by to enter. From the experience of the project, it would seem that it has succeeded in its attempt to inhabit the commercial flux without becoming a part of it, resisting reductive assimilation. However, several problems soon arose, linked to the architectural options. The lack of a separate reception area meant that the mediator had to greet new visitors in the actual projection space, disturbing the viewers who were already there. In addition, the minimal soundproofing subjected users to the aural disturbances from the shopping centre's PA system and its announcements of special offers. This was a major annoyance for viewers absorbed in the artwork.

After its creation in 2002, the programme alternated between solo and group shows, often as extensions of the exhibitions at Tarbes art centre. Looking back, we can measure the quality of the work done by the curators directing the space, who invited important contemporary artists. Another question that arose concerned the space's flexibility, its capacity to adapt to the production of specific works. Often, Vidéo K simply served as a screening space that was not very different from the usual black boxes. The ambition behind the project, however, had been to offer an adaptable space that would encourage viewers to enter actively into the work. In a text about the project, Yann Chateigné expressed this idea very clearly, 'Entering Vidéo K, going behind the scenes, the viewer becomes an actor: the architecture too, is a

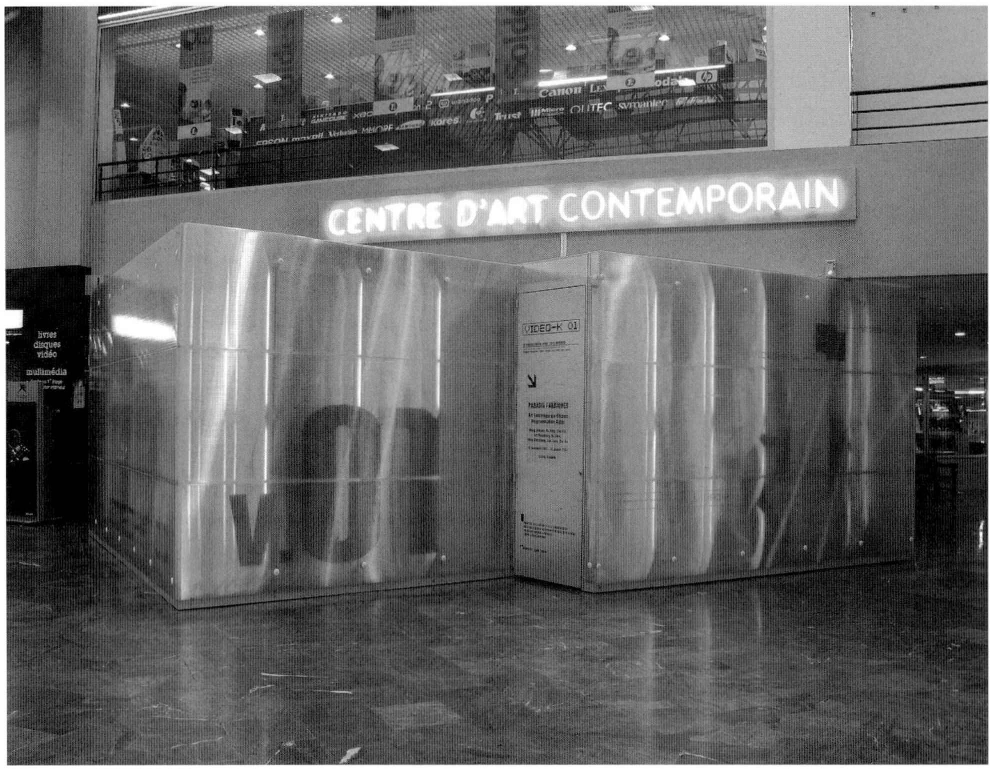

Vidéo K.01. Le Parvis art center, Pau. Photo: Alain Alquier. Courtesy of Claire Petetin, architect.

stage in its own right. Like a "bandstand," a stage open "onto the material setting of life," it is the space of a game that offers "practices" rather than simple uses.[14]

The terminology of spectator and actor is problematic, as we shall see below, but I think, it is above all out of phase with the reality of the experience afforded by the structure. Statistics show that visitors spent very little time in front of the projection, generally between five and ten minutes, and did not return to it, even if they expressed the wish to do so. The organization of special events for schools and students and other groups improved the quality of visitor reception, but in a way unconnected with the space's location in a shopping centre. Furthermore, and contrary to the original intention, the project was not repeated in other locations. No doubt, the difficulty of making the consumer into an attentive viewer has something to do with this. In late 2011, the structure was taken down at the request of the shopping centre, a decision that met with no resistance from either the project initiators or the public. Vidéo K was discreetly withdrawn and there is little likelihood that it will ever be re-installed. Another space on the upper floor has been set aside for exhibitions as well as literary activities. It is more effectively protected and separated from the flux of commercial activity.

The case of Vidéo K is symptomatic of the failure met with by many attempts to get outside art's assigned places, to displace creativity into areas where it is accessible to other publics. But there is something to be gained from analysing its ambitions and failures. Let us hope that it will not be completely forgotten. Partly because of its geographical situation away from the main cities, it was not given the attention it deserved, even from those with a special interest in the visibility of video in public space. It was important, therefore, to mention it here.

Didier Faustino, Artist and Designer

Didier Faustino (France, 1968) is an artist, architect and scenographer, whose multiple activities are all concerned with the exploration of space in relation to the body, and with the energy of performance, in the tradition of Vito Acconci. Trained as an architect, Faustino's projects centre on the body's intimate relation to social space, manipulating perceptions and creating distortions of the body image. Faustino's pieces oblige the viewer to take part in a game that often turns into a trap: bending to enter a minimal space (one square metre), clambering up to a platform to find a surprising tea room, placing their mouth into a double mask that puts them in a disturbing face-to-face with their neighbour. As an exhibition designer, working through the 'Bureau des Mésarchitectures', Faustino speaks to the bodies of exhibition visitors in the same way, taking an interest in the positions of reception and the codes and technical imperatives that condition the relation to the works. The question of constraint, both physical and symbolic, is central. It is therefore not surprising that he has been chosen to elaborate designs for the exhibition of videos with complex requirements.

In 2007, the video collection of Jean-Conrad and Isabelle Lemaître was exhibited at La Maison Rouge, Fondation Antoine de Galbert, in Paris, under the title 'A Vision of the World'. The Lemaîtres are great champions of video art and have brought together works by artists of different nationalities who all offer an incisive, caustic view of the world and

Didier Faustino, 'Une vision du monde, videos from the collection Lemaître'. La Maison Rouge, Paris, 2007. Courtesy of Bureau des Mésarchitectures.

human relations. Faustino's exhibition design spread over the spacious floor area like an aldehyde, an organic compound containing the group –CHO.

Its geometrical structure made it possible to combine open and closed projection spaces, to propose different positions of reception while affirming the overall unity of the ensemble. Even when isolated in a cell, viewers were aware of being part of one big structure in which each element was inseparable from the whole. The power of the exhibition structure was due, in large part, to the plurality of relations to the image that was proposed, in that it associated cinematic-type apparatuses, monitors and installations, as was the case with *Park*

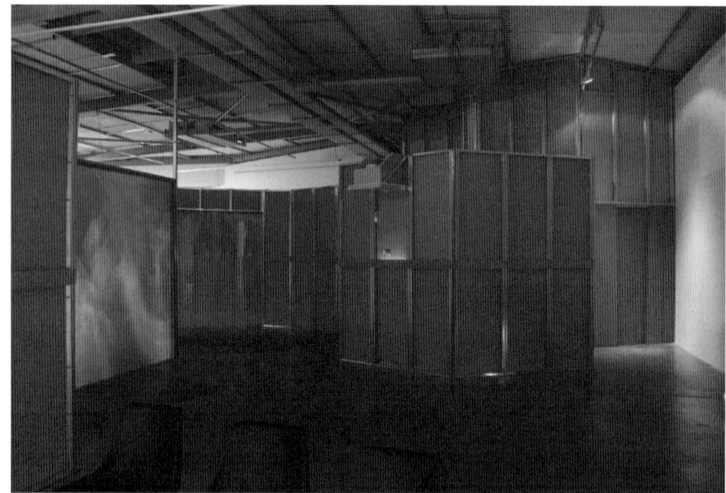

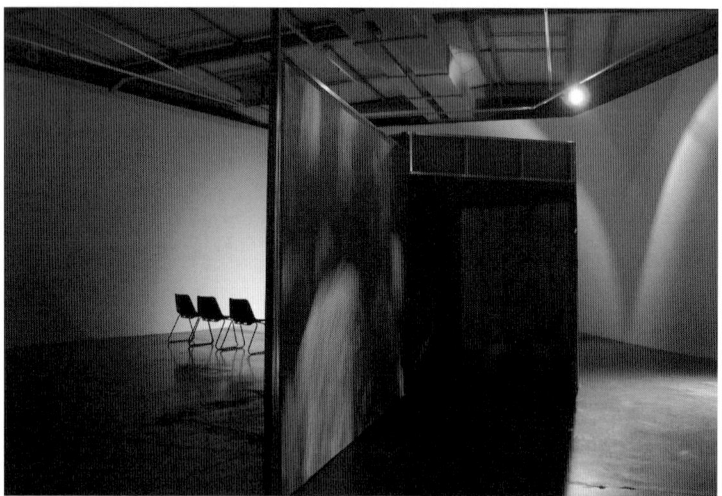

Didier Faustino, 'Une vision du monde, videos from the collection Lemaître'.
La Maison Rouge, Paris, 2007. Courtesy of Bureau des Mésarchitectures.

by Aernout Mik (2002). Finally, Faustino replaced the traditional black curtains closing off the projection rooms with heavy strips of red plastic.

The effect was extremely surprising. The management of the sound was effective while visual contact was maintained between outside and inside: viewers remained conscious of being in a group show, and psychological immersion in the work resulted from active attention. The modest materials used for the exhibition sets also conveyed the idea of a transitional, ephemeral state, imaging an immaterial artistic form that constantly needs the flux of light in order to be seen. Entering the exhibition, visitors were faced simultaneously with several works, all drawing them into disorienting visions of the world that were sometimes unsettling and always fascinating, enjoining them not to settle down too comfortably there, to continue their exploration, not to stop where they were. This state of mind was of great interest to Benjamin Weil[15], the curator whom Hermès contacted to conceive the *Hbox* project. It was he who decided to bring in Faustino.

The Hbox project

In 2006, before the creation of the Fondation Hermès, Pierre-Alexis Dumas, the company CEO, decided to launch a project that would give visibility to the company's previously discreet artistic patronage. Weil suggested the creation of a mobile video theatre coupled with a programme of producing new works. By deciding to concentrate on young artists and on a form that was easy to transport, the *Hbox* allowed Hermès to express values of nomadism and movement that are important to its brand culture. Asked to design this structure, Faustino came up with a futuristic form that could fit easily into temporary installations in museums, art centres and biennials.

The *Hbox* looks like a spaceship moored on the ground, a UFO that has come there by accident. It declares that its presence is temporary. Open to the exterior, thanks to its entrance ramp, without the opaque curtains that usually close off projection spaces, it rises to the challenge of facilitating audience contact with contemporary videos. Attractive, intriguing and welcoming, it invites us to cross its threshold and find out what is going on inside. The problem that then arises concerns duration: the small interior space, which can hold only ten people, does not encourage them to stay there for as long as is necessary if they are to become immersed in the works, especially when the *Hbox* is installed in places with large visitor numbers such as the Forum of the Pompidou Centre in Paris. The constant flux of visitors coming and going, the queue of waiting spectators, all make it difficult to become immersed in the works. In such a setting, the *Hbox* becomes a space of circulation, inducing viewers to engage in a certain kind of creative nomadism, to grasp the initial idea behind the project. As Benjamin Weil points out, the point was in effect to bring together artists 'who all have a poetic vision of the world. They are themselves nomads, working in different cities'.[16] The mobility of viewers encounters the state of mind of the makers of these productions. A framework that is possible only because the works all have short formats.

The constraints imposed by the *Hbox* on one side, and on the other, the financial investment from Hermès, enabling each artist to produce a new work, provide an ideal

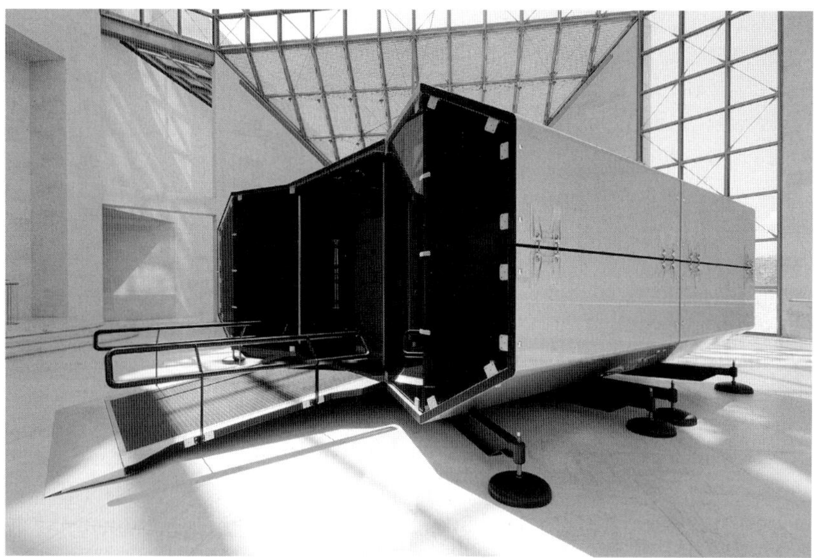

Didier Faustino, *Hbox*, 2006. Installation view at Mudam, Luxembourg. Photo: Andres Lejona. Courtesy of the artist and Hermès.

context for works questioning their projection space. *Oracle* (2007) by Sebastian Diaz Morales, a montage of footage from the artist's travels in Europe, Asia and South America, was a perfect fit for the *Hbox* by virtue of its non-narrative nature and its topographic drift. The differences between the filmed landscapes become meaningful, thanks to the subjectivity of the vision and the soundtrack, which immerse the viewer in a gentle ambulatory movement. In contrast, *Bluebeard* by Alice Anderson (2007) fitted less well because its structure is such that it needs to be seen in its entirety. The *Hbox* works particularly well for showing short cyclical works, playing on effects of repetition, like *A banda dos 7* by Sara Ramo (2010), or *Open Score* (2007) by Su-Mei Tse. In the latter work, the artist films herself in a small white room, suggestive of the white cube, playing a game that resembles squash. Su-Mei Tse faces the camera, dressed in city clothes, and hits a ball against the walls with what looks like a tennis racket, in slow motion and with increasing temporal distortions. Rather than a game against oneself, *Open Score* is an absurd movement back and forth, disconnected from the physical effort (the artist is never out of breath) and the world of sport in general. Attention soon focuses on the noise of the ball bouncing, the sound of a space at once closed and strangely distended. A feeling of unease gradually develops, making viewers aware of their own relation to space–time, and of their false solitude.

Didier Faustino says that he was trying to offer 'an experiential architecture in which the body becomes a sensitive film and a hyper-sensorial receiver'.[17] The aim is to integrate the body into the projection, to offer an immersive situation in which viewers entering the vessel themselves become active in the process of reception. The title plays with the idea of the black box, to which it evinces a relation by responding to a number of constraints associated with the presentation of videos in open spaces (providing the necessary darkness and insulation of the sound) while at the same time dissociating itself from these by maintaining an openness onto the outside. The structure of the *Hbox* explores the idea of movement, from a transitional state in which the viewer is also encouraged to place themselves. This investigation connects with the work of experimental filmmakers such as Malcom Le Grice and Tony Conrad in the 1960s, who combined multiple projections with live performance, and with a disjunctive treatment of time. As Duncan White very aptly points out in an article about the period, 'instead of being used to synchronize time and space, to make it unified, linear and continuous, the time of viewing intervenes; it breaks up the film time'.[18] These devices broke with cinema's historical status as an art that combined time and space in the movement of images and the running of the soundtrack. The fragmentation of the image in space is a privileged tool for challenging narrative schemas, for rethinking the position of the viewer and deconstructing the time of the film. While the *Hbox* is not designed for the creation of installations or the specific handling of its space, because it was made for collective programmes, it is nevertheless a space where viewers engage in a particular relation to the projected images.

Tobias Putrih: Towards a Total Exhibition Experience

As a child, Tobias Putrih (Slovenia, 1972) grew up in a Yugoslavia marked by the Communist ideology, as reflected in the organization of collective life, urban development and architecture, but came of age in an eastern Europe that was transitioning away from socialism, and in a new state, Slovenia, that came into existence in 1990. History is central to his concerns, and manifests itself in a variety of ways. After training at the Academy of Fine Arts in Ljubljana and at the Kunstakademie in Düsseldorf with Tony Cragg, Putrih soon began to focus on the memory of modernism, using poor materials (cardboard, polystyrene, chipboard) to build models, objects and spatial installations that assert a sense of fragility, a relation to the ephemeral, and using irony and lightness to institute a sense of distance with regard to the functionalism of design and architecture.[19] His historical reflections are manifested through the analysis of forms and the re-appropriation of the architectural utopias of the early twentieth century in sculptures that annex the space of the museum. Aware of the importance of the exhibition space in the way we perceive work, and in the emergence of an imaginary, he builds large-scale installations that question modernism, in a manner that establishes him as an heir of Kurt Schwitters and his *Merzbau*. Like Schwitters, Putrih often hosts work by other artists in his installation, taking an interest in architecture as a support for display.

Cinemas occupy a central position in his work. While a great deal of critical analysis has been devoted to the architecture of museums and galleries and its effect on the perception

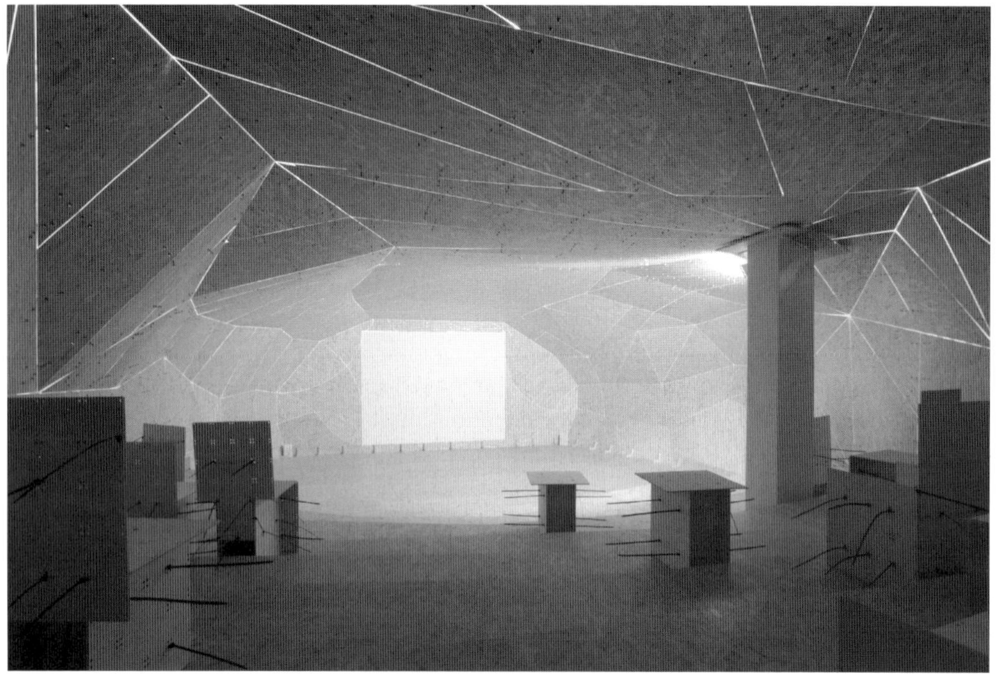

Tobias Putrih, *Cinema attitudes*, Genève, 2008. Courtesy of the artist and Attitudes art center.

of artworks, from the early days to the now much-contested white cube, the structure of movie theatres has been relatively ignored. And yet, the history of their organization is closely bound up with the evolution of relations to power and to the image.[20] Putrih creates projection spaces that affirm their materiality and formal stance, and that therefore remain present in the way we look at the works. Viewers remain aware of the place occupied, of the structures surrounding and immersing them in a particular environment. In Putrih's installed cinemas, spectators enter genuine sculptures and can watch the projection without losing sight of the materiality of the support that makes it possible.

Putrih has created several cinema rooms inside exhibition spaces, always seeking to inscribe the film image, whatever its nature, in a dialogue with the ephemeral structure. Some of his projects have been designed for programmes decided elsewhere; others have clearly articulated the structure and the film(s) presented inside. The approach is simple and clear: 'My idea is to provide a space where films can be projected'.[21] However, as we have seen, putting such projects in place in a museum can be complicated. In 2008, Putrih created a large structure made up of pieces of pressed wood for the *Cinéma Attitudes* show at Attitudes—Espace d'Arts Contemporains in Geneva. Exhibiting the supports of its construction, the outside of this piece was covered in scaffolding and cleats crudely nailed into the wooden boards. Inside, simple benches were laid out, pierced by long and cumbersome cable holders that hampered movement but were not strictly necessary. Visitors, who moved through this strange volume towards the screen, could not put the setting out of their mind. The programme established by this cinema was inscribed in a dense visual environment that could not be ignored. The works screened there all involved a reflection on architecture, and were thus coherently articulated with Putrih's sculptural proposition. Even when absorbed by the projection, visitors remained aware of the space, recalled at every moment by the discomfort of the benches. This is in line with Putrih's insistence on avoiding the kinds of space where the spectator 'gets rid of his own body'.[22] In Putrih's cinema, the gaze is constructed through a plurality of sensations and in an environment that reaches beyond the edges of the screen.

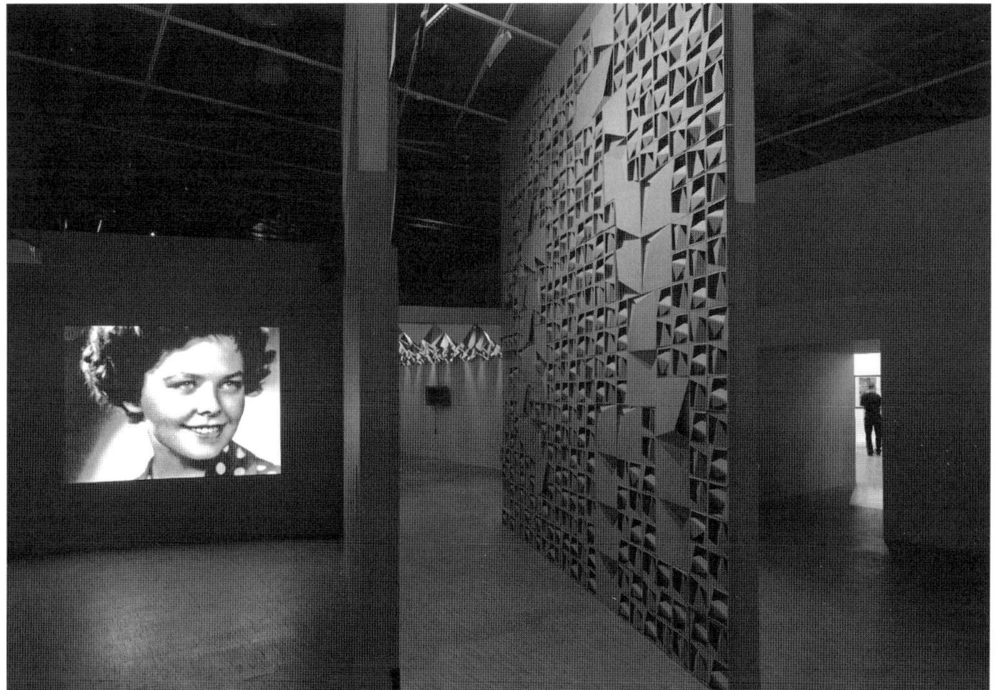

Tobias Putrih, *Šiška International*, 2010. Espace 315, Pompidou Center, Paris. Photo: Georges Mèguerditchian. Courtesy of the artist and gallery Gregor Podnar, Berlin.

The curators of the exhibition *Les promesses du passé* (Centre Pompidou, 2010),[23] about the art scene in socialist (pre-1989) Eastern Europe, built their approach around the idea of historical discontinuity, and the circulation between generations and artists in East and West. They asked Putrih to design a space for showing archive footage and videos and films. His starting point here was his own childhood memories of a local cinema in Slovenia, one whose architecture and interior decoration were emblematic of Soviet modernism. Years later, Putrih found a cinema with very similar features on Karl Marx Allee in Berlin, also built in the late 1950s and featuring an extensive glass façade. His proposition, *Šiška International,* was based on a reflection on the conception of these cinemas, on the way these big foyers leading to the auditoriums opened onto the street, and on their geometrical ornamentation. As Zdenka Badovinac recalls, 'These buildings had no secret corners, just like the alleys of the big socialist cities, which were subject to constant surveillance'.[24] By choosing to develop this project inside the Pompidou Centre, Putrih was adding another layer of meaning because this host space also plays on the ideal of transparency, albeit this time in the name of democratic openness. In the appropriation that he proposed with *Šiška International,* he replaced the transparency of glass with the obstructiveness of cardboard, introducing a sense of openness by cutting out forms and including lighting. He put false ceilings in a structure that did not have any, hiding the pipes that are part of the Pompidou Centre's image, shrinking the volume and partitioning off the floor area. It would be reductive to see this as no more than an evocation of the old political contrast between an open and transparent Western Europe and an isolated Eastern Europe cut off from the outside world. On the contrary, it constituted an ironic reversal of the trust that is all too easily accorded to what is exhibited, to what is given to be seen, the better to hide. With the kind of glass architecture found in many other museums, such as the Fondation Cartier in Paris, the Pompidou Centre exemplifies this belief. Exhibiting its structure to all, offering curious passers-by a glimpse of its ground floor rooms, it plays with the idea of a museum for all. Putrih's structures took the opposite position, calling into question this use of transparency that reveals only to better exclude. As in *Shadow Piece* by David Claerbout, glass structures exclude the body even though they are penetrated by shadows and the gaze. In *Šiška International,* tubes and cones filled the space, leaving comfortable projection areas but strongly shaping perception of the environment. In complete contrast to the white cube, this complex space, with its intensely worked cardboard corridors, left a paradoxical impression of both precariousness (the material) and finesse (the cutting thereof). Within the museum, the space of cinema became a place that one looked at; its materiality did not immediately recede behind its use. This is what interests Putrih, who always seeks to draw out the moment when the setting of the projection is noticed, to make it fully a part of the experience of the film. What interests him about the model of cinemas with glass façades, which we will discuss further in relation to Dan Graham, is its contradictions: rather than opening onto the street, onto the real, the cinema is a space of confinement within fiction, of the disappearance of the body and space. By creating invasive cinematographic layouts in the museum, Putrih tries to resolve this tension by making the experience of receiving films a moment that is at once spatial and temporal; to reconcile two separate logics for, as he points out, 'the choreography of the museum visit is spatial, whereas that of the cinema is temporal'.[25] In his propositions, the viewer is immersed in a spatial and temporal reception, in a gaze that forgets neither the space where it is located nor the representation facing it.

The Projection of Gazes: Perceptual and Psychological Issues

To reflect on the context of the projection, to imagine spaces and supports for the video experience, is to raise the question of perceptual habits. The works that invent apparatuses engage the subject in new experiences that bring into play the relation to the world sustained by the relation to images. Artistic experience becomes the place of an immersion that affirms our situated being, that is to say, the non-isolation of the perceiving consciousness. The subject is in the world, caught up in the flux of sensations, at once perceiving and perceived, constantly reminded of inter-subjectivity, broadening our vision of the world to the presence of others. By questioning the image, and doing so through perceptual spatio-temporal experiences, the works of Dan Graham and Laurent Grasso occupy territories of thought strongly marked by phenomenological philosophy.

Dan Graham: Broadening Perception, Multiplying Gazes

Since his first works in 1965, Dan Graham (United States, 1942) has developed a corpus informed by the analysis of perceptual phenomena, combining performance, video, photography and installation. His pieces are interested in the body's relation to its visual, architectural and aural environment, and through this to symbolic, individual and collective frameworks that structure our sense of self and relations to others. His performances thus put the viewer at the centre of the action, playing with their perception.

Performer/Audience/Mirror (PS1, NY, 1977) is divided into seven scenes in which Graham stands between a mirror and the audience, questioning his reflection. His body becomes an image, engaging the public. In scene 1, he concentrates on his own corporeal movements, describing them from an outside viewpoint ('the body moves'), trying to define them as closely as possible, to apprehend them with great spatio-temporal precision, but also to understand their meaning. His awareness of moving around in a theatrical context, defined by the presence of an audience and a camera, determines his relation to speech, but also raises problems.

> (…) and I'm walking… walking in this direction towards the wall of the room off the stage: the movement stops on the word 'stage'.

The interruption marks the unsettling effect of being confronted with the theatrical model. Performative displacement suddenly comes up against theatrical vocabulary, defining the space of the action as a stage. Graham becomes still, making visible the complexity of performance's relation to the stage. Caught up in the presence of the action, he is carried by the feeling that he is at one with the audience that is sharing the same time frame. This spontaneity produces 'a theatrical effect that underscores the performance'.[26] But the point is that Graham tries to call into question the obvious power of the action's theatricality, and its breaking-off when the word 'stage' is spoken marks his distance from a model of representation whose codes he prefers not to espouse. His words now go about bringing out the gap between himself and the audience. As of scene 2, he thus describes the actions and postures of the audience during scene 1. In this way, he introduces a temporal and visual discrepancy between what is seen, what is heard and what is perceived: 'The position of the audience is different from mine, they can see that my description comes after the event, that my interpretation is different from theirs'.[27] The sensation of belonging to the same present is thus disrupted by awareness of the different viewpoints on the same situation. Graham undermines the theatrical effects in order to show up the very framework of perception, to make the public conscious of its condition as an audience facing the performer.

This action followed on from *Performer/Audience Sequence* (1974), in which Graham was already alternating between the description of his own person and that of the audience facing him. As things went on, the descriptions began to mix because, as Graham retrospectively commented, 'my perception of the audience seems to come closer to the self that I project towards it; we are each part of each-other's self-description. Like the politician, the artist here becomes an 'ideal self' with which the mass of spectators identifies, someone who makes their identity meaningful'.[28] Graham thus reveals the systems of co-dependence structuring the construction of identity. By alternating the object of the description (his reactions and those of the public), Graham makes visible the mechanisms of perception, pointing up their psychological aspects and exploring the way in which public representation partakes of a political management of individuals.

Graham's work has also developed a meditation on architecture and the structures that determine our relations to collective space. He is particularly interested in the history of theatre and its modern offshoots, television and cinema. In his text 'Theater, Cinema, Power',[29] he considers the genealogy of theatres and gardens, showing how their architecture embodied and helped to consolidate different conceptions of power. He analyses the way in which Baroque theatres extended the hierarchy and organization of gazes in monarchic society. This text followed a first project from 1981: the conception of a cinema (which never got beyond maquette phase) revealing the subjective and collective functioning of vision in the framework of an immersion in cinematic fiction.

His *Cinema* was meant to be installed on the ground floor of a modernist office building occupying the corner of a street. The external wall is a two-way mirror, so that passers-by can observe the movements of spectators entering the projection room, sitting down and waiting for the beginning of the film, then getting up and making for the exit. During the projection, the luminosity of the screen made it possible to see the silent gathering captivated by the film, instituting a face-to-face between two kinds of viewers equally compelled by an appearance of images. In an article on this work, Gregor Stemmrich shows its links to the film theory developed by Jean-Louis Baudry, which contrasts two conceptions of the cinema screen, as 'window' and as 'mirror'.[30] This reversal, which Baudry bases on Lacan's theory of the mirror phase, integrates the viewer's experience in the movie theatre within the framework of the

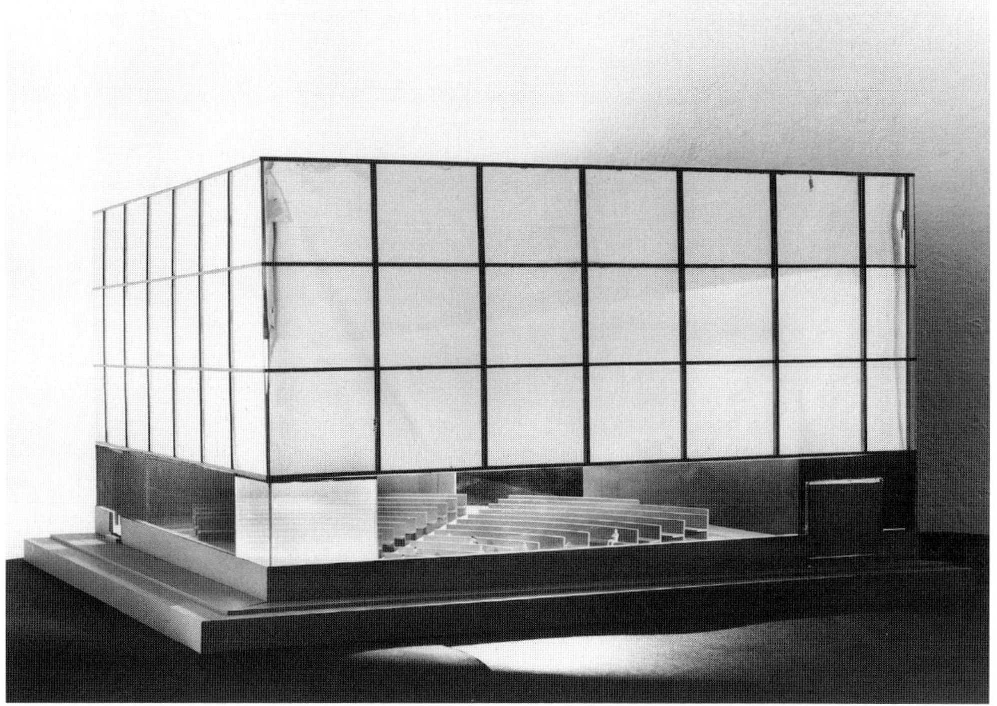

Dan Graham, *Cinema*, 1981. Foam-core, wood, two-way Mirror plexiglas. Super 8 projector and super 8 film. Courtesy of Dan Graham Studio and gallery Marian Goodman Paris/New York.

analysis of a film. The technical apparatus used for projection and the psychological content of the experience within a collective space are asserted as the elements constituting the reception of an artwork. In the same line of ideas, Graham's *Cinema* analyses the importance of the spatial context in which a cinematographic work is seen. Even if the film immerses the viewer and isolates them in an individual experience, the viewer nevertheless maintains a connection with those experiencing it at the same time. The cinema is a place of assembly, an activity that people take pleasure in sharing, from the expectancy before the screening to collectively leaving the theatre afterwards. Back in the street, the viewer is torn between lingering emotions from the film and the return to reality, with these two things clashing or merging, depending on the state of mind provoked by the film.

In *Cinema*, Graham shows the importance of the context in which a film is received, and uses the circulation of gazes to make visible the individual and collective psychological function of an art that is too often analysed in terms of its images alone. The point for Graham is to make the conditions of their immersion, the mechanisms of illusion, perceptible for the spectator, and to underscore the theatrical heritage behind the architecture of cinema.[31] The cinema interior proposed by Graham is thus based on the arena model, with the seating

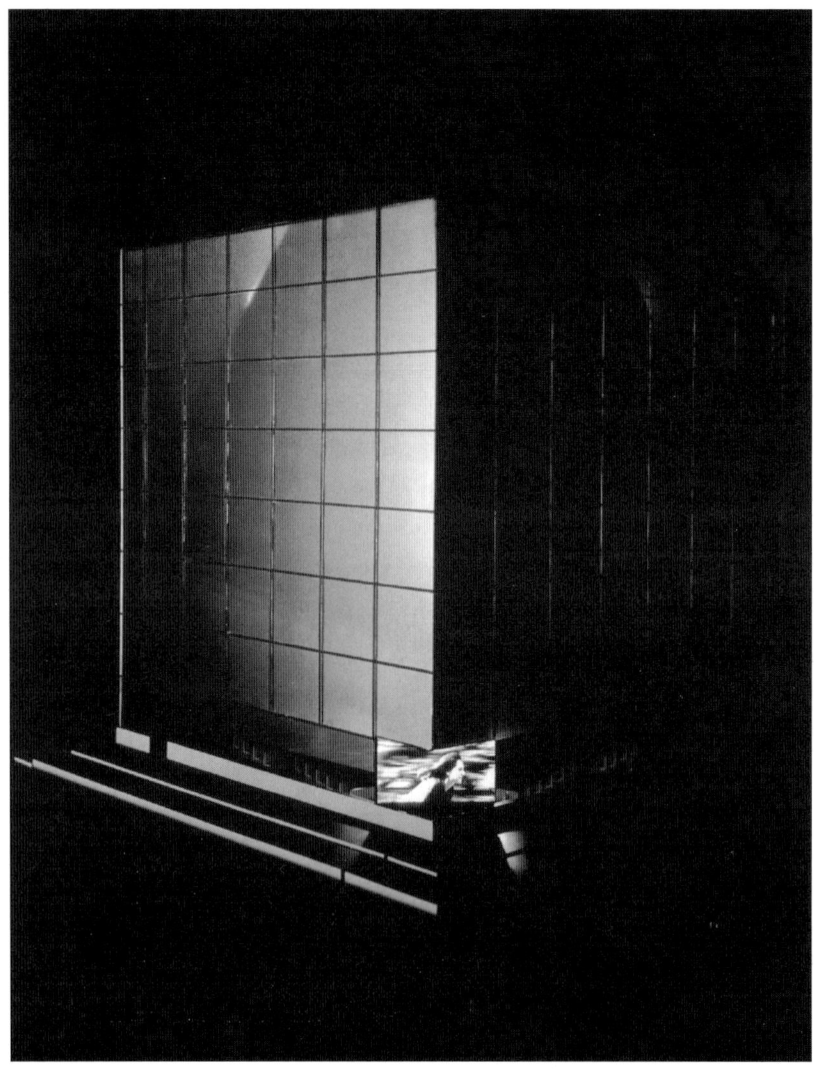

Dan Graham, *Cinema*, 1981. Foam-core, wood, two-way Mirror plexiglas. Super 8 projector and super 8 film. Courtesy of Dan Graham Studio and gallery Marian Goodman Paris/New York.

around the room avoiding the frontal relation to the screen, which in this case, stands in the middle of the space, surrounded by rows of viewers. In the tradition of the *Teatrum Mundi*, *Cinema* marks the proximity between what appears on the screen and what happens in the street, taking us from one to the other in a single gaze. As in Baroque theatres, where the audience watched both the actors on stage and the king up in his box, in an image of the social hierarchy outside, Graham's *Cinema* makes visible the mechanisms of seeing in democratic states. From the cinema theatre, we observe the spectacle of the world, not through a *mise-en-abyme* of illusion and reality, but through the association of the twin experiences of the spectator of fiction and the spectator of seeing.

However, while *Cinema* offers the combination of an external and an internal gaze, Graham does not make them one and the same thing. On the contrary, he highlights the differences in the psychological mechanisms of vision in accordance with the place where it is constructed: 'The position of the outside observer can be distinguished from that of the interior, seated spectator. The outside observer does not relinquish his consciousness of self or awareness of environment for the (silent) movie image. Further, he is free to move around the sides of the theatre and remove himself from the cinematic illusion in order to obtain a general, outside perspective on the audience-film relationship'.[32] In fact, the position of the outside viewer described by Graham is that of the viewer of a video installation, freed from the frame of cinema, invited to move around the work, to let them be drawn in and decide on the duration of reception. It is by exiting the architecture of cinema, deploying its other side, making visible its optical and symbolic functioning, that Graham anticipates the state of the viewer moving around a museum space inhabited by numerous projections.

Cinema and Graham's studies of the 1980, summed up in 'Theater, Cinema, and Power', inspired the German theoretician and gallerist Rüdiger Schöttle to write 'Bestiarium: Theater and Garden of Violence, War and Happiness',[33] relating an imaginary visit to a Baroque garden that synthesizes the architectural history of theatres, melding reality and fiction, past and future. The model, inspired by the cinema auditorium, stands on a big table where maquettes dialogue with images and sounds. This principle was the starting point for a group show curated by Chris Dercon, *Theatrum Bestiarum: The Garden as Theater as Museum* (1989). The artists brought together here were invited to reflect on the idea of the theatre of memory. Several projects appropriated the structure of the theatre stage. Models/sculptures by Rodney Graham, Marin Kasimir and Juan Muñoz questioned the place of representation, its architecture and the management of the gaze. Walking around a dark room amidst large tables on which works were placed together, all lit by the slide projectors hanging from the ceiling, spectators became aware of the interplay between what is shown and what is hidden, between what is perceived and what escapes the gaze (as in *The Prompter* by Juan Muñoz), between what is understood and what remains enigmatic. *Valor Impositus* by James Coleman, a small pile of bones half gathered together in the form of a human skeleton reflected in a blue cube, highlights the element of construction needed for the real to be recognized and identified, and for a pile of bones to impose the vision of a vanitas.

This piece partakes of Graham's ongoing analysis of the workings of perceptual mechanisms. His contribution consisted of a more elaborate version of the *Cinema* architectural model, titled *Cinema=Theater*, and this time comprising not only the projection room on the ground floor of a glass building but also, on the other side of the screen, a theatre with Baroque architecture open onto an antique arena. The film projected, *The Rise to Power of Louis XIV* by Roberto Rossellini (1966), echoed Graham's text 'Theater, Cinema, Power', in which he analyses Rossellini's staging of the political management of the gaze by Louis XIV through the elaboration of court rituals and the construction of the Château de Versailles. The architectural model sums up the long history of representation, creating a link between the ruins of antique theatres, the stage of a Baroque-type theatre, and the contemporary movie theatre. Actors are on a stage in front of the screen, seeming to replay, in turn, the court's comedy of mores in front of an absent audience. The different places of representation raise, above all, the question of the viewer's omniscience, installed in front of the stage and film images, as an heir to the pyramidal organization of gazes of which Louis XIV is an emblem here.

The viewer of the *Theatergarden Bestarium*[34] faces an exhibition/installation that stages a history of representation by showing the unified organization of the visible. All the pieces reference the model of perspective, its symbolic and political sway, while walking round the space offers very different conditions of perception. The height of the tables, the semi-darkness throughout, and the lack of labels all create a state of uncertainty: it is difficult at first sight to tell the works apart and to identify their makers. Placed together on trays covered with sugar, they acquire a collective unity that is heightened by the projections: the images are not identifiable but create haloes of light and colour that bathe the pieces. Greeted by Graham's maquette, viewers enter immediately into a reflection on the space of reception and its codes, leading them to experience the destabilization of the places of representation. We witness a symbolic dispersion, requiring active commitment from the viewer. In a text about this project, Frédéric Migayrou shows how the *Theatergarden Bestiarium* 'never defines the garden as a framework or stage for a demonstration in which everyone would have to choose a place, a position. If there is a stage, then it is established only as the extension of a constructive reception of each work'.[35] The conceptual unity of Schöttle's project is counterbalanced by the fundamental autonomy retained by each piece, making it necessary to find the appropriate receptive position each time. The hierarchized uniformization produced by the architecture of Baroque gardens and theatres is, as Graham points out in his catalogue text,[36] found nowadays in theme parks and events, where the image plays a very important role. This exhibition, with no video pieces as such, was put on at a time when projections were becoming extremely widespread in museums, often combined with theatrical apparatuses for viewing them. By pointing to the symbolic mechanics that can soon confine gazes and immobilize thoughts, it deserves to stand as an important moment in the reflection on projection spaces. Contrary to the screens that place the viewer in a relation that is often immobile and captive, the screen in *Theatergarden Bestarium* is, according to Schöttle's description, like 'an artificially agitated ocean, an ocean forever creating new conceptions by means of countless images that keep emerging and submerging'.[37] In contrast to the screen that rises above the gaze, he emphasizes the idea of a screen that appears below, that floods vision only to later become lost in the meanders of memory. Moving over a shifting expanse of mixed impressions, the viewer settles into a multiple and open mode of perception.

The installations later conceived by Graham for showing his videos within exhibitions extend these reflections on the organization of gazes and the receptive state of the public with regard to moving images. He thus conceived transparent modules that isolate the viewer from ambient noise while maintaining their visual contact with the exterior. These structures allow viewers to enter into videos while remaining aware of their relation to images. There are several versions of this apparatus, each one consisting of a glass or pierced metal structure creating autonomous spaces in which the monitors are laid out. Spectators can sit down and concentrate on a work while retaining their visual contact with the room. In a play of mirrors, they perceive other visitors also engaged in an intimate relation to the screen, returning to the everyday framework of the relation to television.

However, every time the gaze strays away from the video image, the view of other spectators points to the subject's own immersion and makes them fully aware of it. The experience of Graham's work is built around this reflection of gazes, this back and forth between the seeing and the seen. The ghostly reflections of the viewers' bodies mix with the bodies facing the monitors and the bodies in the film, creating a state of uncertainty. The viewer has no set place, nor is there a dominant viewpoint. Everything is in a state of constant reversal and communicates in a constant probing of the relation to images.

Throughout his work, Graham has always sought to avoid the loss of awareness that, as he sees it, characterizes psychological immersion in cinema, when the viewer yields to illusion. Wary of such effects for symbolic as well as political reasons, his work uses innovative apparatuses in order to ground the gaze in a consciousness of the conditions of perception. Exploring different projection structures, reversing perspectives, his influential spaces of experience and meditation have a significant contemporary heritage. Cited by many younger artists as an example, he was a precursor in his exploration of the porous relations between cinema, video and theatre. If the ensemble dialogues and communicates to such magnificent effect in *Cinema=Theater*, and if we are compelled by the interaction between the transparency into which gazes are absorbed on the one side and the opacity that stops them on the other, this is, above all, because this construction designates a regime of the visible and a history of the management of gazes. Artistic power is underpinned by a philosophical progress stimulated by readings of texts related to phenomenology and political issues.

Laurent Grasso: Displacing the Places of Illusion

The work of Laurent Grasso (France, 1972) flirts with the supernatural, drawing on the potentially cinematic and fantastic dimension of the real. Video and 3D animations are the tools he uses in his fertile dialogue with cinema. The apparatuses he creates to project his films and present his sculptures are works of art in their own right, designed to create unique states of receptiveness by combining disorientation with sensorial stimulation. A good example is his 2004 exhibition *Radio Ghost* at the Credac, a contemporary art centre in Ivry-sur-Seine, south of Paris. The venue itself is particular; formerly a basement cinema, it has a sloping floor and no windows. For *Radio Ghost*, Grasso played on the history of the venue by creating a projection booth where visitors could isolate themselves and enjoy a view down onto the images projected in the room, showing aerial views of Hong Kong filmed from a helicopter, reducing the city to the scale of a model. Inside, a soundtrack comprised the words of the technicians working for Hong Kong radio and cinema, recalling paranormal apparitions witnessed during shoots. These left the viewer in a state of expectation; the apparitions described here would have been taken as part of the fiction if they had been placed within the narrative, but they were hard to credit when placed outside the field of the projection. With this piece, Grasso took viewers into the workings of the radio and cinema industries, revealing a world where the frontier between the real and the surreal is porous. The narratives were recorded in Hong Kong and not in Los Angeles, and naturally, this location also showed how a given culture has appropriated an imported art form. Here, the films of Apichatpong Weerasethakul come to mind, which clearly show the importance of the belief in ghosts in Thai culture, and film in a very natural way the communication between the living and the dead in everyday life. The stories heard in *Radio Ghost* are rooted in a belief in wandering spirits but also echo the many attempts made by spiritist circles at the beginning of the twentieth century to decrypt the interference observed during broadcasts on electromagnetic waves.

By positioning the viewer in the space of the technicians, Grasso displaces the locus of fiction and questions the narrative content of his production tools. He makes visible his means of production but, rather than using it to distance illusion as Dan Graham does, he continues to manipulate it, albeit by shifting it to other territories. By presenting the narrative in the projection booth, a highly symbolic space where the production of illusion comes into play, he causes a productive mutual contamination of the real and the imaginary. Viewers then affect a back-and-forth movement between the two spaces, walking from the booth to the gallery, never leaving the fiction. The images of Hong Kong, which have a particularly strong impact when viewed in the projection booth, take on a very different meaning when they are combined with the ghost stories. What we lose when leaving the cinematic apparatus is turned into an even more disorienting experience related to the margins of fiction. Two opposing visions, one external and objective, the other intimate and subjective, dialogue and question both the places that are filmed and the codes of representation.

Grasso's pieces are always presented with special techniques of immersion whereby viewers are at once lost in the image and aware of their movements. In one interview, he stresses on the importance of inscribing the artist's experience in space, 'Like everyone, when I move through an exhibition I like to feel displaced, sent elsewhere, disconnected, to construct a situation, a space–time Framework. (…) There is always something hypnotic about my installations, in my films that helps me at any moment "block" the spectator, or better to slow him down, to offer him something else'.[38] The projection of videos in an exhibition space is thus an integral part of a reflection on perception and on the construction of a vision. Grasso aims to provoke a specific relation to images by conceiving architectural structures that truly accompany the fiction. His position may seem to go against the grain of the research done in the early twentieth century to shift the viewer from a passive to an active state. Slowing things down and creating blockages are not the most obvious ways of encouraging active reception. Grasso pauses the process whereby the viewer projects into the fiction and makes them lose their perceptual bearings, but also structures his pieces so as to introduce a sense of uncertainty about the status of what is being shown. Often, it is hard to know what we are supposed to be seeing in the pieces before us; we do not know what we should believe and perception becomes troubled. Access to the works and to their meaning is deliberately diffused and the points of entry are half concealed.

Projet 4 Brane (2007) extends these questions in relation to another locale, that of a projection module. From the outside, the viewer is confronted with a dark, reflective monolith, close to minimalist sculpture. It would be easy to walk round it without noticing that there is an opening cut into it, giving onto a small room where artists' videos are shown. This proximity to the minimalist aesthetic is interesting, in that, as we have already noted, the experiments made by Robert Morris and Tony Smith were key moments in the shift towards theatricality in the relation to the exhibition space. When faced with *Projet 4 Brane,* as with the sculptures of John McCracken, the viewer is at first made aware of their own movement

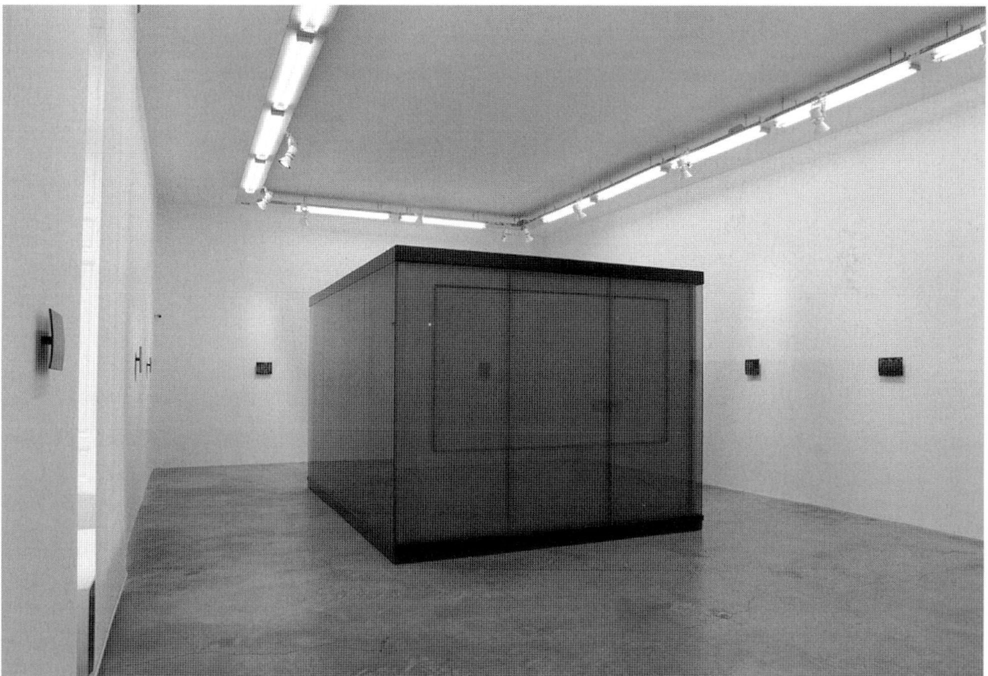

Laurent Grasso, *Projet 4 Brane*, 2007. Exhibition view, Perrotin Gallery, Paris, 2014. Courtesy of the artist and Perrotin Gallery.

around the exhibition, reflected in the appearance of their image on the structure's surface. This experience thus leads them to define their position in a space, to affirm their presence in relation to the work, before noticing, as they approach the perforated iron and respond to the variations in luminosity, that there are other viewers inside the module. They will then seek to enter it in order to become immersed, in turn, in the spectacle produced by the moving image.

These videos are not Grasso's own, and the programme is re-thought for each new exhibition. The module was not made, therefore, to accompany one artwork in particular; it is not sculptural prolongation of the explorations conducted by the image, as in video installations, even if intelligent programming can throw up some richly meaningful echoes between the videos and the structure. This was the case with *Chambres, conversations* (2006), a video by Dora Garcia about the encounter between a Stasi officer and a civilian informer. This narrative took full advantage of the play on opacity and transparency and viewer and viewed in Grasso's piece. In a generic way, however, *Projet 4 Brane* is conceived more as a small exhibition cinema, an heir of the little movie theatres now found in every museum. Far from being merely a structure for showing, though, it is also a sculptural object that is there to be seen as much as it allows us to see. The material used links it both to the

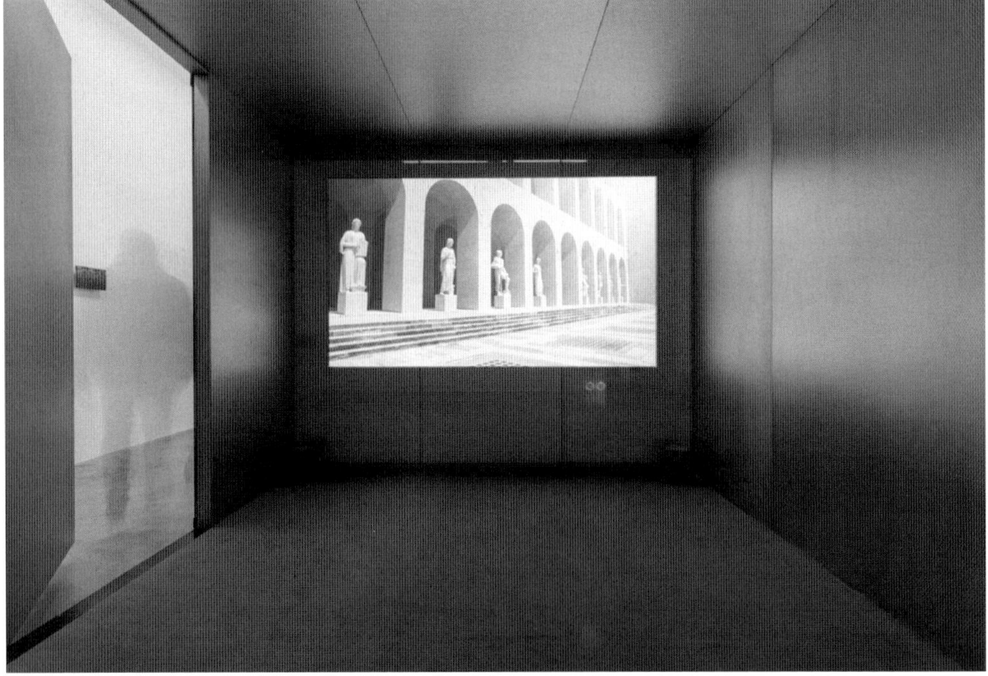

Laurent Grasso, *Projet 4 Brane,* 2007. Exhibition view, Perrotin Gallery, Paris, 2014. Courtesy of the artist and Perrotin Gallery.

picture walls in David Claerbout's exhibitions, which are also perforated, and to the walls of Dan Graham's structures, which alternate between transparency and opacity. Viewers thus remain aware of their presence in the exhibition space, in a collective environment. They knew that they are both the object and the subject of the gaze. In black box-type set-ups, viewers are completely isolated in a cinematic fusion, losing their spatio-temporal bearings in the present. Here, they are cut off from the outside world in order to enter into the fiction, while remaining aware that they are moving around a large exhibition space. They literally disappear into the work but remain at the centre of the circulation of gazes.

The title *Projet 4 Brane* refers to string theory, which is a way of setting up a dialogue between two systems, general relativity and quantum physics, which are equally vital to scientific research but cannot be applied conjointly. Grasso seeks to give us an experience of this fundamental, problematic incoherence through his installation, a point Vanessa Morisset makes very clear in her article on the piece: 'Through the play of transparency set up by the glass and perforated metal of the construction walls, he effectively traces a sequence that is first of all visual, then tactile, and that guides us through heterogeneous spaces. He thus transposes scientific concepts into our world by extrapolating their paradoxes'.[39] More precisely, it is interesting that the coexistence within the same structure of mutually irreducible temporalities, those of sculpture and video, also makes it necessary to find a string theory whereby they can be reconciled. In his title, Grasso plays on the permanent conflict arising from the presence within the same space of works with very different statuses, compelling museums to call into question their own architecture and exhibition structures. The solutions usually found, as we have seen, rarely go beyond constructing a black box in the exhibition space, or the programming of films in an adjoining room, and all too often this fails to convince. The merit of Grasso's *Projet 4 Brane* is that it inscribes the viewer in a dialogue with the exhibition of which the work is a part, avoiding the trap of confinement and encouraging a rereading of minimalism that highlights its role in introducing spatio-temporality into the relation to art. Without becoming dependent (Grasso insists on the work's autonomy, refusing the idea that it is completed by reception), it welcomes and invites the spectator to enter another kind of temporality.

Duchamp's interest in the fourth dimension and his attempts to make it visible in pieces like *A Mile of String* are not very far away here. For the opening of the 'First Papers of Surrealism' exhibition organized by André Breton in New York in 1942, Duchamp hung a multitude of strings in the space and invited children to come and play with balloons, literally preventing viewers from seeing the paintings. He humorously created a device for obstructing vision, thwarting the habitual positions from which the artwork is appreciated. Viewers were hindered in their movements in relation to the works, their attention disrupted by the children's cries, their movements hampered by their games and by the threads. Duchamp's interest in spiritism and esotericism, which were highly fashionable at the time, and in literary and scientific speculation about the fourth dimension,[40] also suggests that this intervention should be understood as an attempt to block the spectators' movements and incite them to develop other sensibilities for gaining access to the work.

Beyond the provocative effect of such an intervention in 1942, *A Mile of String* designates the exhibition space and distances the dominance of visual perception in the experience of art by emphasizing the tactile and the aural, the presence of play and the mental investment needed to attain the meaning of a work. *Projet 4 Brane*, while allowing us to see the works in much better conditions, also probes the complexity of inhabiting a space, of installing a vision that goes beyond the visible. The solution proposed develops the inter-space of sculpture and video, affirming the theatrical dimension of the exhibition of moving images. The dimension of temporality, which, according to the theory of relativity, leads to the fourth dimension, is the fundamental change proposed by the experience of contemporary art. With *Projet 4 Brane*, Grasso affirms its importance while asserting the difficulty of installing this new spatio-temporal grounding within the perceptual framework inherited from the long history of art. By placing great emphasis on olfactory, aural and corporeal devices at the openings of the Surrealist exhibitions that he organized, Duchamp understood the need to displace the locus of illusion by introducing the temporal dimension, and thus unsettling the foundations of perception. Grasso's pieces also experiment, taking an interest in states of the real whose identity is elusive for us. *HAARP* (2009), a big installation comprising eighteen antennae and cables among which visitors are encouraged to walk, represents an American scientific and military research installation in Alaska. The title as well as the scale of the piece suggests a subjacent activity invisible to the naked eye, one that we may hope to get a sense of by walking around it. We cannot determine what belongs to the infra-thin here and what is simply fantasy, what has to do with scientific research and what is part of a great conspiracy. The sense of the world's strangeness that runs through Grasso's work leaves us in a state of uncertainty. As with Duchamp, irony and the manipulation of the viewer's expectations are central, and hypotheses abound.

The question of the *dispositif* (apparatus) is highly important for Grasso as a way of reflecting on representation and on the control structures at work in contemporary societies. The choice of the HAARP base as the starting point and the importance of the size of Grasso's installations are aspects of an ongoing reflection on the spatial and temporal codes that govern our relations to the world. Viewers feel unable to get a grip on the images, sculptures and sounds around them, whose status and workings they cannot precisely ascertain. As with *Projet 4 Brane*, they are constantly pulled between what is going on inside and what is going on outside, between what is visible and what escapes perception and, on leaving, they wonder if, somewhere along the line, they have not missed a point of ingress. Installing and exhibiting video images thus becomes a way of questioning perceptual phenomena, but also challenging the political organization of the visible.

Notes

1   However, the Jeu de Paume does very regularly put on solo shows by artists who use video and devise highly interesting installations to present their work in this medium. Jordi

Colomer and Eija-Liisa Ahtila are two recent examples discussed here, as are Aernout Mik, Laurent Grasso and Natasha Nisic.

2   Roland Barthes, 'Leaving the Movie Theatre', *The Rustle of Language*, University of California Press, 1982, p. 408. p. 346.

3   Dominique Païni, *Le temps exposé. De la salle au musée*, Éd. Cahiers du Cinéma Essais, 2002, p. 71.

4   A.L. Rees, Duncan White, Steven Ball and David Curtis (eds.), *Expanded Cinema. Art, Performance, Film*, London: Tate Publishing, 2011.

5   'On the Development of Snows and Other Early Expanded Cinema Works', Carolee Schneemann interviewed by Duncan White, New York, April 2008, op. cit., pp. 85–90.

6   For a detailed analysis of the *Movie Drome* and of Stan Vanderbeeke's work generally, see, the article by Mark Bartlett, 'Socialimagestics and the Visual Acupuncture of Stan Vanderbeek's Expanded Cinema', op. cit., p. 50–61.

7   Published in *Film Culture*, vol. 40, 1966 and reprinted in *Expanded Cinema. Art, Performance, Film*, op. cit. p. 80–84.

8   Interview given in May 2011.

9   From Gerry Schum's introductory words to the *Land Art* programme produced in 1969.

10   Not having been able to experience this installation, my analysis here is based on descriptions.

11   By way of an introduction to his book of interviews with artists and experimental filmmakers, Doug Aitken states that he wants to 'challenge the assumption that disorientation is dangerous and to propose that the randomness we encounter in life can be very productive', *Broken Screen, 26 Conversations with Doug Aitken,* d.a.p., 2006, p. 8.

12   Atelier FAT Design, Atelier van Lieshout and Claire Petetin.

13   'Le Vidéo K: la maison aux images', Claire Petetin, *Vidéo K*, éd. le Parvis centre d'art contemporain, 2004, p. 14–23.

14   'Vidéo K. 01', Yann Chateigné, *Vidéo K*, op. cit., p. 33–34.

15   Benjamin Weil became artistic director of the Centro Botín in Santander, Spain, in 2014.

16   Quoted by A.-M. Fèvre in his article 'Hbox, de l'art dans la boîte Hermès', *Libération*, 5 December 2007.

17   Quoted by A.-M. Fèvre in his article 'Hbox, de l'art dans la boîte Hermès', *Libération*, 5 December 2007.

18   'Degree Zero: Narrative and the Contextual Image', Duncan White, *in Expanded Cinema.* op. cit, p. 118.

19   'The fragility of the architectural models and design prototypes related to these explorations is simply a way of keeping things under control as much as possible, of preserving their intimate aspect and the imminence of their collapse, in case people failed to understand their irony or took them too seriously'. Tobias Putrih interviewed by Anna Hiddleston, Cambridge, Mass.-Paris, 02.2010, in *Tobias Putrih Šiška International*, Éd. Centre Pompidou, 2010, p. 17.

20   See the analyses by Dan Graham, which will be discussed in detail below.

21   'Lost Cinema Lost', Runa Islam and Tobias Putrih, Modena, Italy. Tobias Putrih interviewed by Milovan Farronato, 2008.

22   *Movie Tales*, press release by Gregor Podnar gallery, 2001.

23 Curators: Christine Macel, Joanna Mytkowska and Nataša Petrešin-Bachelez for 'Sources, documents, films, archives' space. 14 April–19 July 2010.

24 *Šiška International*, by Zdenka Badovinac, in *Tobias Putrih Šiška International*, Paris: Ed. Centre Pompidou, 2010, p. 23.

25 Tobias Putrih interviewed by Anna Hiddleston, Cambridge, Mass.-Paris, 02.2010, op. cit., p. 17.

26 'Ma position', in *Ma position. Ecrits sur mes œuvres*, Dan Graham, éd. Le Nouveau musée/ Institut, Presses du réel, Villeurbanne, 1992, p. 98.

27 'Ma position', in *Ma position. Ecrits sur mes œuvres*, Dan Graham, éd. Le Nouveau musée/ Institut, Presses du réel, Villeurbanne, 1992, p. 98.

28 'Ma position', in *Ma position. Ecrits sur mes œuvres*, Dan Graham, éd. Le Nouveau musée/ Institut, Presses du réel, Villeurbanne, 1992, p. 43.

29 Dan Graham, 'Theater, Cinema and Power', *Parachute* (Montreal), no. 31, June-August 1983, p. 11–19.

30 Gregor Stemmrich, 'Dan Graham's *Cinema* and Film Theory', in *Art of Projection*, Stan Douglas and Christopher Eamon, Hatje Cantz, 2009, p. 93–110. The text by Jean-Louis Baudry is 'The Ideological Effects of the Basic of Cinematographic Apparatus', in Gerald Mast et al., *Film Theory and Criticism: Introductory Readings* (New York and Oxford, 1992), pp. 302–312, quoted by Gregor Stemmrich, id.

31 Cf. 'Theater, Cinema, Power', Dan Graham, in *Dan Graham: Rock my Religion; Writtings and Art Projects*, Cambridge, Mass.: Brian Wallis, 1983.

32 'Cinéma, 1981', *Ma position. Ecrits sur mes œuvres*, Dan Graham, éd. Le Nouveau musée/ Institut, Presses du réel, Villeurbanne, 1992, p. 158.

33 This text is part of a series of essays under the general title *Psychomachia*, begun in 1979.

34 Held by the CNAP in Paris, before that, this piece has been in several exhibitions curated by Guy Tortosa.

35 Frédéric Migayrou, 'The Stage and the Register', *Theatergarden Bestarium, The Garden as Theater as Museum*, Cambridge, Mass.: MIT Press, 1990, p. 67.

36 Dan Graham, 'Garden as Theater as Museum', *Theatergarden Bestarium, The Garden as Theater as Museum*, op. cit., p. 86–104.

37 Rüdiger Schöttle, 'Bestiarium: Theater and Garden of Violence, War and Happiness', *Theatergarden Bestarium, The Garden as Theater as Museum*, Cambridge, Mass.: MIT Press, 1990, p. 11.

38 *Radiodays, what happens when viewers become listeners?*, Onestar Press, 2006, p. 36–37.

39 Vanessa Morisset, 'L'ombre d'un doute. Science et réalité dans l'œuvre de Laurent Grasso', *20/27* n° 2, 2008, p. 169.

40 Marcel Duchamp refers to the writings of the mathematician Poincaré and the speculative novel by Gaston Pawlovski *Voyage dans la quatrième dimension*, 1912.

Conclusion

On Stage: From Exhibition Space to Mental Space

The introduction of temporality into visual artworks plays on the sense of a meeting that involves the viewer in the encounter with the work. The mobility of the gaze and the movements of the body ground the experience in a spatio-temporality that runs counter to the purported neutrality of the exhibition space. The importance for museums of scenographic questions relating to the presentation of the moving image—in the end, it matters little whether the format is video or film—arises from this increased focus on the reception space. Revisited or imagined modalities of projection and installation explore the history of our relations to images and re-appropriate and question the models of cinema and television,[1] but they also arise from experiments with screens in the performing arts. Indeed, numerous video artists have worked on stage projects, among the most illustrious being Bill Viola, Gary Hill, William Kentridge and Pierrick Sorin. By accepting the constraints of live performance, the frontality of the viewer's relation to the work and the limitation of duration, they affirm the basic connection between the video image and the stage space. Projected on the stage, its status is no different, and that is what explains the difficulties artists have in truly displacing their work and integrating it into a stage show, be it musical, choreographic or theatrical. Now, without deterritorialization, there is a great risk that the change of locus will not be accompanied by new conditions of reception, which would lead to disappointment and boredom.[2] The point of affirming the theatrical dimension of the projected image is not to encourage confusion between the stage and exhibition contexts, but to analyse the way in which certain qualities of theatrical works have been assimilated by contemporary practices of the installed image.

Immersion in such installations makes viewers aware of their perceptual habits and the role played by their body and gaze in the reception of an artwork. If installations often play with immersive and participative registers, in this book I've preferred to focus on works that make use of known perceptual models while introducing displacements that bring to light the symbolic schemas underpinning them. The projection screen is thus placed at the centre of the relation to the work, its materiality affirmed and even transformed in the cases of Jordi Colomer and Mika Rottenberg into a fully fledged sculptural installation. A volume of essays, *Screen/Space: The Projected Image in Contemporary Art*, analyses this phenomenon attentively and includes, notably, an essay by Kate Mondloch on Michael Snow in which she brings out a modus operandi that is shared by multiple installations.

She writes, 'Screen-reliant installations such as Snow' grapple with (at least) three screen spaces simultaneously: the space behind the screen, the space before the screen, and, finally, the spatial presence of the screen object itself'.[3]

Moving through an image that is expanded in space,[4] the viewer's perceptions are challenged as they are pulled into an experience in the present, but they do not become an actor: the *mise-en-abyme* is more mental than corporeal, as we have shown with regard to the works of David Claerbout and Laurent Grasso. The title of this book, *On Stage*, does not mean that the viewer literally comes on stage, that they perform the work, but that temporality is henceforth a constitutive dimension of the aesthetic relation, and that for the artist the theatrical space is a partner in the same way as the exhibition space. As Elie During shows in his analysis of *Present Continuous Past(s)* by Dan Graham, 'the prestige of the *dispositif* is clearly not enough to transform a spectator/subject into a the "performer" of a video installation'.[5] Even if, as in this work, viewers enter a pavilion where, in spite of themselves they become participants in a continuous performance that disrupts the relation to time and to self-image, they are still not actors of this transformation. During prefers to call them 'erratic operators of their own subjective experience'.[6] The vocabulary of wandering crops up recurrently when talking about works in which the viewer is temporally immersed in the exhibition space. It serves to designate the multiplicity of possible experiences, the non-linearity of the sequence, the required affective and mental receptiveness, and above all, the position of non-mastery imposed by contact with the work. To say that the beholder, when moving through the exhibition, is 'the operator of their own experience' is to position them as executant, as cameraman of their vision. It is on this basis that, in the moment of immersion in the work, they can be made conscious of their perceptual condition. Far from acting in the space of the work, they are acted by it.

Liberated from the fantasy of interactivity, from the belief that the spectator is transformed into an actor of their experiences of vision through the process of active reception, the video installations and projection apparatuses discussed here approach the exhibition space in a way that affirms its theatrical dimension. The connection with the history of theatre is evident in artists' frequent use of the terms 'stage', 'set' and 'performance' and in the emphasis on the 'present' of the experience. But there is also a clear and deliberate distance: the confrontation with the work does not take place within a standardized architecture, as is still often the case in theatre, where the seats are distributed in keeping with a social hierarchy and an economic power that contribute to the political organization of the gaze. On the contrary, in the exhibition, the space is open to different circulations, to mobile positions. It is a place where pathways are multiple, where the durations of experience can be modulated in keeping with each person's receptiveness and desire, in which speech can accompany reception. It is the time of rehearsal, of experiment that takes place on stage in a closed theatre, more than the time of public performance. It is a time of tentativeness with moments of doubt and illumination, solitude and collective enthusiasm, inwardness and confrontation with what is happening. James Coleman in *Retake with Evidence* (2007), Jordi Colomer in *Les Jumelles* (2001) and Maïder Fortuné with *Curtain!* (2008)—three pieces discussed here—explore this metaphor by taking over the temporal and spatial margins of theatrical representation. The work takes place without needing viewers to be there, and then they enter it, they witness what happens on stage outside the duration of the show. Their movements through the exhibition space give rise to a mental representation in which their every step makes more uncertain the frontier between the front and back of the screen, between the person looking and the person being seen. With *Rocking Chair* (2003), David Claerbout thus creates a silent encounter between the viewer and an old lady hidden in the shadow of her house, rocking in the chair. Her face appears when the viewer moves round the screen and discovers a frontal view of the character. In this work, Claerbout provides an experience that is symptomatic of the relations that the projected image sets up with the viewer: opening up perspectives, multiplying viewpoints and making the gaze conscious of its own wandering.

Notes

1 Maeve Connolly offers a very precise analysis of these questions in *The Place of Artists' Cinema. Space, Site and Screen*, Bristol and Chicago: Intellect Ltd, 2009.
2 This was the case, for example, in the Peter Sellars production of *Tristan and Isolde* with Bill Viola in 2005.
3 'The matter of illusionism: Michael Snow's screen/space', Kate Mondloch, in *Screen/Space: The Projected Image in Contemporary Art*, Manchester University Press, 2011, p. 85.
4 Here I am echoing the term 'expanded cinema.' Cf. chapter 3.
5 Elie During, *Faux raccords, la coexistence des images*, Actes Sud/Villa Arson, Arles, 2010, p. 85.
6 Elie During, *Faux raccords, la coexistence des images*, Actes Sud/Villa Arson, Arles, 2010, p. 85.

Bibliography

Aitken Doug, *Broken Screen. 26 Conversations with Doug Aitken*, d.a.p., New York, 2006.

Baker George, *James Coleman*, Cambridge, Mass.: The MIT Press, 2003.

Barthes Roland, 'Leaving the movie theatre', *The Rustle of Language*, California: University of California Press, 1982, p. 346.

Bellour Raymond, 'Le "Film" de James Coleman', *Trafic, D'un autre cinéma*, Paris, summer 2000, no. 34, p. 5–21.

Berg Stephen, Franke Anselm, Gregos Katerina, and Thorp David, *Julian Rosefeldt Film Works*, Ostfildern, Germany: Hatje Cantz, 2008.

Besson Jean-Louis (ed.), 'L'acteur entre personnage et performance. Présences de l'acteur dans la représentation contemporaine', *Centre d'Études Théâtrales*, Louvain-La-Neuve, Belgique, 2003, no. 26.

Bronfen Elisabeth, Durand Régis, and Krystof Doris, *Eija-Liisa Ahtila*, Ostfildern, Germany: K21 Hatje Cantz, 2008.

Claerbout David, *The Shape of Time*, Zürich: JRP/Ringier; Paris, France: Éditions du Centre Pompidou, 2009.

Coleman James, Fisher Jean, Buchloh Benjamin H.D., and Cooke Lynne, *James Coleman, Projected Images: 1972–1994*, New York: Dia Center for the Arts, 1995.

Colomer Jordi, 'Habiter le décor', *Pavillon*, 2009, Monaco, no. 2, p. 62–71.

Colomer Jordi, *Fuegogratis*, Cherbourg, France: Le Point du Jour/Jeu de Paume, 2008.

Connolly Maeve, *The Place of Artists' Cinema. Space, Site and Screen*, Bristol and Chicago: Intellect Ltd., 2009.

David Catherine and Dercon Chris, *Hélio Oiticica*, Galerie Nationale du Jeu de Paume, Paris, and Witte de With, Rotterdam, the Netherlands,1992.

Dercon Chris and Schöttle Rüdiger (eds.), *Theatergarden Bestarium, The Garden as Theater as Museum*, Cambridge, Mass.: The MIT Press, 1990.

Douglas Stan and Eamon Christopher (eds.), *Art of Projection*, Ostfildern, Germany: Hatje Cantz, 2009.

During Elie, *Faux raccords, la coexistence des images*, Arles, France: Actes Sud/Villa Arson, 2010.

Falguieres Patricia, 'Aire de jeu', *Les Cahiers du Musée National d'Art Moderne*, Paris, autumn 2007, no. 101, p. 48–71.

Fernandez Laure, 'L'espace dramatisé de l'installation vidéo: *The Chittendens* de Catherine Sullivan, une autre scène pour le théâtre', *Figures de l'art n°18, L'œuvre en scène ou ce que l'art doit à la scénographie*, Pau, France: Presses Universitaires de Pau, 2010, p. 102.

Fevre A.-M., 'Hbox, de l'art dans la boîte Hermès', *Libération*, 5 December 2007.

Filipovic Elena, *Tobias Putrih: 99-07*, Zurich, Switzerland: JRP Ringier, 2008.

Foster Hal, *The Return of the Real*, Cambridge, Mass.: MIT Press, 1996.

Fried Michael, *Art and Objecthood: Essays and Reviews*, Chicago: University of Chicago Press, 1998.

Graham Dan, *Two Way Mirror-Power: Selected Writings by Dan Graham on His Art*, Cambridge, Mass.: MIT Press, 2000.

Graham Dan, *Rock My Religion: Writings and Art Projects*, in Brian Wallis (ed.), Cambridge, Mass.: MIT Press, 1983.

Graham Dan, 'Theater, Cinema and Power', *Parachute*, 1983, Montreal, no. 31, p. 11–19.

Grasso Laurent, *Le rayonnement du corps noir*, Dijon, France: Presses du Réel, 2009.

Jauss Hans Robert, *Toward an Aesthetic of Reception*, Minnesota: University of Minnesota Press, 1982.

Kitnick Alex, *Dan Graham*, Cambridge, Mass.: MIT Press, 2011.

Lageira Jacinto, 'Le syndrome de Vélázquez', *Parachute*, 2001, Montreal, no. 103, p. 72–85.

Lauraire Héloïse, 'Ugo Rondinone, Roundelay', www.mouvent,net. Uploaded 12 March 2003.

Lehmann Hans-Thies, *Postdramatic Theatre*, Oxford: Routledge, 2005.

Macel Christine, *Tobias Putrih Šiška International*, Paris, France: Éditions du Centre Pompidou, 2010.

Mondloch Kate, *Screens. Viewing Media Installation Art*, Minneapolis, Minn.: University of Minnesota Press, 2010.

Mondzain Marie-José, *Homo Spectator*, Paris, France: Bayard Presse, 2007.

Morisset Vanessa, 'L'ombre d'un doute. Science et réalité dans l'œuvre de Laurent Grasso', 2008, no. 2, p. 163–75.

Païni Dominique, *Le temps exposé. De la salle au musée*, Paris, France: Cahiers du Cinéma Essais, 2002.

Parenzan Giovanni, 'La colonne relevée', Agôn (online), no. 2: L'accident, Dossiers. http://w7.ens-lsh.fr/agon/index.php?id=1062. Uploaded 16 December 2009.

Peletin Claire, *Vidéo K*, Tarbes, France: Le Parvis Centre d'Art Contemporain, 2004.

Perez Rubio Agustin and Schuppli Madeleine, *Ugo Rondinone, The Night of Lead*, Zurich, Switzerland: JRP/Ringier, 2010.

Picon-Vallin Béatrice, 'Les dispositifs vidéo en question: histoire et actualité', *Pavillon*, 2011, no. 3, p. 28–37.

Picon-Vallin Béatrice (ed.), *La scène et les images*, Paris, France: CNRS Arts du Spectacle, 2001.

Rees A.L., White Duncan, Ball Steven, and Curtis David (eds.), *Expanded Cinema. Art, Performance, Film*, London: Tate Publishing, 2011.

Rosefeldt Julian, *Living in Oblivion*, Bielefeld, Germany: Kerber Art, 2010.

Ryngaert Jean-Pierre and Sermon Julie (eds.), *Le personnage théâtral contemporain: décomposition, recomposition*, Montreuil, France: Editions Théâtrales, 2006.

Sobieszczanski Marcin and Masoni Lacroix Céline (eds.), *Du split-screen au multi-screen. La narration vidéo-filmique spatialement distribuée*, Bern, Switzerland: Peter Lang, 2010.

Snow Michael and Dompierre Louise, *The Collected Writings of Michael Snow*, Waterloo, ON: Wilfrid Laurier University Press, 1994.

Staebler Claire, *Radiodays, What Happens When Viewers Become Listeners?*, Paris, France: Onestar Press, 2006.

Trodd Tamara (ed.), *Screen/Space: The Projected Image in Contemporary Art*, Manchester: Manchester University Press, 2011.

Van Assche Christine, *Collection Nouveaux Medias Installations*, Paris, France: Éditions du Centre Pompidou, 2006.

Index